TIM CONDER

THE CHURCH IN TRANSITION

The Journey of Existing Churches into the Emerging Culture

FOREWORD BY DAN ALLENDER

ZONDERVAN™

GRAND RAPIDS, MICHIGAN 49530 USA

ZONDERVAN.COM/
AUTHORTRACKER

ZONDERVAN™

The Church in Transition: The Journey of Existing Churches into the Emerging Culture
Copyright © 2006 by Tim Conder

Youth Specialties products, 300 South Pierce Street, El Cajon, CA 92020, are published by Zondervan, 5300 Patterson Avenue SE, Grand Rapids, MI 49530

Library of Congress Cataloging-in-Publication Data

Conder, Tim.
  The church in transition : the journey of existing churches into the
emerging culture / by Tim Conder.
      p. cm.
  ISBN-10: 0-310-26571-1 (pbk.)
  ISBN-13: 0-310-26571-5 (pbk.)
  1. Church renewal. 2. Christianity and culture. 3.
Postmodernism--Religious aspects--Christianity. I. Title.
  BV600.3.C67 2006
  262'.001'7--dc22

                                                                    2005024204

Web site addresses listed in this book were current at the time of publication. Please contact Youth Specialties via e-mail (YS@YouthSpecialties.com) to report URLs that are no longer operational and replacement URLs if available.

Creative Team: Doug Davidson, Laura Gross, Brad Taylor, Mark Novelli, and Heather Haggerty
Cover design by Holly Sharp
Printed in the United States of America

---

06 07 08 09 10 • 10 9 8 7 6 5 4 3

For Mimi, Keenan, and Kendall

In Memory of Nancy Conder

CONTENTS

FOREWORD   7

INTRODUCTION   11

CHAPTER ONE   17
The Church in a Changing Landscape

CHAPTER TWO   37
Seven Deadly Fears and Seven Essential Conversations,
Part 1: Culture and the Gospel

CHAPTER THREE   59
Seven Deadly Fears and Seven Essential Conversations,
Part 2: Scripture and Ethics

CHAPTER FOUR   77
Seven Deadly Fears and Seven Essential Conversations,
Part 3: Christian Traditions

CHAPTER FIVE   95
Changing Your Worship Service:
Why the Obvious Starting Place Is Usually Not the Best Starting Place

CHAPTER SIX   105
Transition in Spiritual Formation

CHAPTER SEVEN   127
Transition in Leadership

CHAPTER EIGHT   143
Transition in Community Formation

CHAPTER NINE   165
Transition in Mission

CHAPTER TEN   189
Transition in Worship: "So What about Worship, Anyway?"

CHAPTER ELEVEN   197
The Journey into the Emerging Culture

ACKNOWLEDGEMENTS

First, I want to thank the congregation and leadership of Chapel Hill Bible Church. Your gracious embodiment of Jesus' kingdom, relentless analysis of cultural realities, and courageous willingness to explore new horizons has created the context for the vision of this book. I owe special thanks to Jimmy Long and Jim Thomas, gifted leaders and friends, who have walked the long and fruitful journey of transition with me for many years.

I also want to thank the community of Emmaus Way that has been formed out of this vision. You've had the faith and boldness to seek to embody the practices of this vision with very few roadmaps and examples. Denise Friesen and Elizabeth Efird have been inspirations, friends, and partners throughout the whole journey. Steven Nicholson has been a partner and a friend in the shaping of this community. Paul Marchbanks carved hours away from the demands of a dissertation and teaching to read and critique this manuscript. Melinda Denton, Don Taylor, Rich Henderson and Scott Vermillion have been confidants and constant encouragers.

My friends and colleagues in Emergent have not only inspired me, but their creative expression of the path of Jesus has given me an irrepressible hope for the future of the church. Thanks so much to Ivy Beckwith, Rudy Carrasco, Jason Clark, Tony Jones, Tim Keel, Brian McLaren, Doug Pagitt, Mark Scandrette, Chris Seay, Holly Rankin Zaher, and many others who have contributed to this community.

My brothers and sisters, Keenan and Debbie Conder, Mebane and Michael McMahon, and Michael and Tony Martin have contributed wonderful stories of faith and ministry as well as beautiful settings for the writing of this book. Daniel Harrell fits the definition of a brother. Our more than two decades of conversation about the church have influenced every aspect of this book. I also want to offer special thanks to my dad, Don Conder, for his life of faithfulness and incessant encouragement.

Thanks to Jay Howver and Mark Oestreicher of Youth Specialties and John Raymond of Zondervan for their vision for this book and for offering me the privilege of writing it. Many thanks to Doug Davidson for his encouraging and insightful editing.

Most of all, I want to thank my wife, Mimi, my son, Keenan, and my daughter, Kendall. Your enthusiasm for this project has been unwavering. You have embodied the vision of this book with the whole of your lives.

FOREWORD

Perhaps it has been said too often and with too little meaning: We live in a transitional age. There are too many variables spinning too rapidly in trajectories that are beyond the existent models of prediction. One only need consider the rise of global terrorism and our inability to capture the most reputed terrorist leaders in spite of our massive infrastructure of surveillance technology and military prowess. We live in a new age, and what we've known as solid and sure are no longer true and valued.

Transitional periods, historically, have given rise to heightened anxiety and trauma. It's as if the boat we've been sailing with confidence has taken on water in the bilge as a storm brews on the horizon. The natural tendency is to turn back and find a safe harbor to weather the storm. When no safe place exists, we—like sailors of the past—often turn to superstition and ritual. We return to what we know and what has taken care of us before.

I believe this is part of the dynamic we face in the church. Our numbers are unquestionably shrinking. In spite of the rise of political power for religious conservatives and the record-breaking sales of apocalyptic novels, the horizon portends difficult weather. George Barna and other researchers tell us that—more than ever in the history of Christianity—for every new convert to the faith, it takes many more in the church to bring that person along to spiritual maturity. Though many today report a faith in God that mirrors the language of the Bible, there is less vitality and sacrifice in the church than existed 20 years ago.

We can't go back, and we can't hold on to old practices as if they will protect us from the uncertainty ahead. We can't keep doing the same old thing for another 30 years and expect the results will magically change. Even if we are terrified and confused, we have to stumble forward and create and reform new models to engage our transitional age.

We may not yet know what we must jettison and what is too precious to leave behind, but we must do something other than holding on to either/or binaries that inevitably bind us to a dogmatic past. We need a guide that will handle the helm as we plunge into the storm.

Tim Conder has offered a glorious vision of how we can steady ourselves with one hand on the past while reaching to the future. Tim is a pastor who has lived in the world of the traditional, biblically solid evangelical church and has also ventured far beyond the safety of the tried and true. He's among the forerunners in the emerging church movement who is navigating the new waters of this age and has not forsaken or forgotten truth and tradition.

Tim is generous, kind, passionate, and humble. Yet he handles the helm with courage and immense skill. I have seldom known a more courageous man.

This book is a primer for the traditional church to become part of a community of transition. It is time to leave the solace and slavery of Egypt for a brave new world where faith is far more than adherence to a set of propositions—yet is no less committed to truth. Tim wisely and kindly invites us to leave the shore and venture into the watery world of an age that requires both tradition and innovation.

I can't imagine a better person to guide us. I can't find a better work that calls us to become a radically new and biblically founded community. I am proud to say Tim is a board member of Mars Hill Graduate School. He is my boss. He is a man I've set sail with to venture as a pilgrim to a new land. I gladly serve him. I believe you will find this book is a vessel that will take you into the storms with hope and the promise of the gospel.

- Dan B. Allender Ph.D., president, Mars Hill Graduate School

INTRODUCTION

I drive a 1993 Saturn sedan with many, many miles on the odometer. The car has been wrecked a few times. Its leather seats are disintegrating. The fabric on the ceiling droops and dangerously obscures the driver's vision. For the past three blazing, North Carolina summers, the air conditioning hasn't worked at all, leading us to dub it "The Sauna."

Despite its many eccentricities, this car is greatly loved by my two kids, as well as a couple of their friends. When I mention the imminence of a vehicle upgrade, my 10-year-old son, Keenan, protests vociferously. Having inherited all of my sentimental genes, he passionately reminds me of all our good memories of driving to soccer and baseball tournaments in "The Sauna." Not only does he want to drive the car when he's old enough, but he also intends to keep it forever.

Keenan's allegiance to our deteriorating family car is a reminder that change can be difficult even when it's necessary—and it can be especially tough when it involves powerful memories, shared experiences, and passionate beliefs. That's one reason why discussions of change and transition in the church often generate such strong emotions.

Of course, the church is much more than an old car that can be sold, stripped for parts, or sent to the junkyard if it no longer runs well or feels comfortable. The church is a living organism, enlivened by the presence of God's Spirit. It's the body of Christ—a community of worshippers that exists for God's pleasure and to live out the kingdom that Jesus preached and promised.

I believe we are living in an era when the church must open itself to change if it would fulfill its calling. Our culture is rapidly moving from a modern, rational, individualistic, Enlightenment society to a world increasingly described as postmodern, post-rational, and post-Christian. The uncertainty of our future is reflected in our use of words like postmodern, post-rational, and post-Christian. We find it much easier to talk about the familiar past than this unknown future. But one thing is clear: Amid the turbulence of this cultural transition, the church faces a time where change is both necessary and inevitable.

There is little doubt that a widening crevice has emerged between the existing church and its surrounding culture. By existing church, I'm referring to the radically diverse mosaic of historic Christian churches—from storied cathedrals to small storefronts, both traditional and contemporary, around the corner and around the world—that currently dominates the Christian world. As we will see, the identity of the existing church has been thoroughly shaped by the assumptions, threats, challenges, and opportunities of modern, Enlightenment culture. Many existing congregations are struggling to find their way amidst the emerging postmodern culture of our day.

Last week, while sitting in our local coffee house, I overheard an animated conversation. With fascination and a hint of sadness, I listened as half a dozen people laughed together about Christian attempts to "save their souls." One person summarized—to the affirmation of the group and many nods around the establishment—that "the Christians are the ones who need to be saved."

As a pastor who has many friendships and relationships outside of the church, I often feel like I'm standing in a dark, deep chasm between two cliffs. On one towering precipice stands the church, with its long history of effective ministry empowered by a passionate faith in Jesus that humbles and challenges me. But atop the other is a radically changed world that reflexively finds the language, idioms, assumptions, and affirmations of the church—when it considers them at all—to be irrelevant, alien, impenetrable, or even oppressive. It's my hope that this book will help existing churches bridge this gap.

Over the past 15 years, I've been privileged to work closely with some of the most creative and gifted visionaries in what is known as the emerging church or emergent movement. I've found deep hope in the efforts of the emerging church to minister in this new cultural environment. I've watched these exciting new forms of Christian community scale this second cliff and begin to discover and embody God's story in the midst of these new realities. While many of these communities are radically different from the more established congregation I served, I've learned much from the thoughtfulness, beauty, and creativity of their expression. I've come to believe emerging churches are plotting out some of the paths of transition that can help existing churches navigate these difficult waters of cultural change.

The founders of the emergent movement never set out to be developers of "cool churches" or even revolutionaries. Although these leaders were once deeply critical of the existing church, in recent years emerging church leaders have moved decidedly from a stance of deconstruction of the existing church to creative and collaborative construction of the future church. This bodes well for the whole body of Christ.

I see many signs of hope and creative transformation within established churches.[1] With each passing day, many congregations—small and large, rural and urban, denominational and independent, liberal and conservative—are starting down the exciting path of transition. As I hear their stories, ideas, and adventures, my confidence in the future of the church grows. New forms of Christian community are being explored, and creative communication and radical embodiments of the ways of Jesus are springing up in many existing churches.

This book is rooted in the great hope I have for the existing church in this time of transition. Looking ahead, in the first chapter we'll pursue the nature of the emerging culture, the explorations of the emerging church, and the issues of transition related to the existing church. I will also share more of my own journey, since my perspective is shaped by my personal experiences.

In the next section, we'll look at "seven deadly fears" that can prevent existing churches from transitioning effectively to the cur-

---

[1] As I typed this sentence, I had the sharp realization of how different this statement would have been even five years ago. That's when I vividly remember sitting at a conference with a church consultant who gently laughed at my then meager hopes for existing church transition. Then just five years later, I heard this same leader offer a powerfully compelling description of the adaptability and future influence of the church in the postmodern age.

rent cultural environment. I feel strongly that the transition of the existing church is not merely about programs and practices. Instead, this journey is about adjustments in thought and theology that accompany the practices of transition. Changes in our worship service or ministry practice run the risk of being inauthentic, shallowly rooted, and short-lived if there's no re-exploration of our theology, with new questions framed from a postmodern perspective and theological issues unearthed in transition. Strong fears and oversimplifications in theological dialogue can short-circuit a transition before it ever begins. By taking a look at these concerns and by inviting existing churches into conversation around the issues that lie beneath the fears and oversimplifications, we pave the way for transition to more effective ministry in the postmodern world.

Then we'll spend a chapter on each of the primary arenas of practice for the church: spiritual formation, leadership, community formation, mission, and worship. As we explore each of these essential aspects of Christian community, we will develop new definitions (and dust off some old ones) as we consider the church's historical narrative and its entry into the emerging culture. Our consideration of these aspects of community life and ministry will be an extension of the theological issues discussed in the previous section. Most significantly, we will explore and expose critical transitions of practice in each of these arenas that facilitate the church's authenticity, credibility, and faithfulness to the gospel of Jesus as it enters the emerging culture.

In the final chapter, we'll explore six pathways of transition that embrace both the theological dialogues and the transitions in practice developed in the previous sections. Each of these pathways will draw on symbols from Israel's journeys in exile and in rest as the community that served as the vehicle of God's mercy for a broken and lost world.

As we consider transition, we should remember that the community of those who follow Jesus Christ has endured many upheavals, reformations, and transitions throughout its history. When we consider our story of faith, we see the Spirit of God guiding the community with pillars of fire; reforming it and sending it out with the Pentecost miracle; nurturing its mission through theological controversies, sordid political associations, and institutional lethargy; and protecting its authenticity despite the arrogant claims and accusations of the modern world. I have little doubt that God's Spirit will guide and protect the church through the postmodern transition and beyond. As in every era of challenge and change, our primary task is to find and to follow the leading of God's Spirit, rather than stubbornly insist on the static paths of comfort and convenience made by our own hands and feet.

CHAPTER ONE

The Church in a Changing Landscape

EMERGING CULTURE, THE EMERGING CHURCH, AND CHURCH IN TRANSITION

Recently, a national newspaper ran a front-page story about a Christian leader who sought to distance himself somewhat from the religious right. He expressed some remorse that he'd chosen political sides earlier in his ministry. Today, in an era when some theological conservatives refuse to share the podium with any who disagree with their views of salvation and theology, this leader now opens his events to sponsorship and participation by the full spectrum of Christianity. "If I took sides in all these different divisive areas," he contends, "I would cut off a great part of the people that I really want to reach." In the article, he carefully explains how the term *evangelism*—presenting the good news of the hope God offers humanity—differs from *evangelical*—the label chosen by some theologically conservative Christians. This leader remains passionately committed to proclaiming the gospel, as he has done throughout his long career. Yet he recognizes that a rapidly changing culture demands new approaches to ministry.

Who is this prominent leader? Perhaps an emerging church or post-evangelical voice such as Brian McLaren? Or a social activist such as Jim Wallis? No. This article was about Billy Graham.[2]

Although Billy Graham's goal to spread the good news has not changed over the last half century, his ministry now exhibits relaxed associations and shifts of method. Graham's subtle adjustments reflect dramatic changes in our culture during this timespan. Billy Graham recognizes that we live in an exciting time of transition and adaptation, where dominant worldviews, philosophies, and even theologies are either yielding or at least making room for a new era. This time of transition into a new cultural era has great implications—both opportunities and challenges—for Christianity and the church.

[2] "The Gospel of Billy Graham: Inclusion," taken from *www.USAtoday.com* posted on May 15, 2005.

THE SIGNS OF CHANGE: THE EMERGING CULTURE

One of my neighbors recently stopped in for a long cup of coffee. As often happens, our conversation turned comfortably toward spirituality and religion. He was raised in the church, yet has often told me of his deep concerns about institutional Christianity. He and his wife and two children are all quite engaged spiritually, and he leads a weekly prayer and meditation group for teenagers in his home. Their family is very involved in local social issues, as well as hunger relief projects around the world. He and I share many of the same values and dreams for our community. And my wife, Mimi, and I have been influenced and motivated by their holistic vision of childrearing. He told me he'd be supportive if his children chose, as he put it, "to follow the teachings of Jesus." But he added that any future forays into Christian community for him or his wife would have to differ greatly from the doctrinal inflexibility and relentless guilt that characterized their childhood church experiences. Despite the pain that surrounds his own church experience and his own interest in Buddhist spirituality, this friend continually encourages friends to attend—and also tries to make community connections for—a Christian community I help lead.

My friend's perspective reveals a deep distrust of institutional Christianity and a gentle rejection of the Christian story as the sole resource for truth and meaning. He and his family are open to a diversity of perspectives and relationships. In reaction to our highly individualized society (dominated by individual rights and consumerism), his family exhibits a strong yearning for community. Holism and social activism take prominent roles in their perspectives and family expectations.

The array of values represented by my friend (community oriented, spiritually seeking, politically active, and open to Christianity but suspicious of the institutional church) demonstrates many of the impulses of a new, emerging culture. Social scientists believe the primary worldview of the last several centuries is yielding to a new worldview and culture. The American consciousness is no longer dominated by a Christian consensus on morality and truth. We're moving from a culture with a single dominant story (the Judeo-Christian metanarrative) to a more heterogeneous "post-Christian" society characterized by numerous, competing stories and rivaling views on ethics and truth.[3]

While interest in spirituality remains high, persons in this emerging culture look to a variety of sources for spiritual meaning. Their spiritual searches often come with a wide range of prejudices (some accurate, others less so) about historical and institutional Christianity. Sadly, rather than seeing the church as the light of the world, many people in the emerging culture see the church primarily in terms of its grave moral inadequacies.

This emerging culture is shaped by a philosophy known as postmodernism, which encourages the pursuit of truth along new avenues of inquiry. According to theologian John Franke, postmodernity interprets truth and reality with predispositions of "finitude" and "suspicion."[4] The postmodern mindset tends to reject global, one-size-fits-all-communities-and-contexts explanations of truth. Since the human ability to know truth is finite, postmodern thinkers tend to be wary of any person or institution that offers or demands a universal and infinite view, suspecting such perspectives are often rooted in a desire to control, manipulate, or even do violence to others.

Postmodernism also explains some of the impulses of this emerging culture. Emerging culture persons prefer spiritual worldviews to the mechanistic and scientific explanations of the previous age's modernism. Though individualism remains a hallmark of American society, in the emerging culture the yearning for community is growing, as community experiences are viewed as a source of truth. The individual objectivity of modernism is yielding to a postmodern subjectivity. The postmodern world is one of local communities, contexts, and explanations. It's a world in which experience can trump objectivity and mystery is more comfortable and trustworthy than certainty.

---

[3] Although the U.S. may not experience a post-Christian society to the same measure as Western Europe (we do have a different history), the signs of a post-Christian world are everywhere.

[4] I am indebted to Franke's work on truth and meaning in postmodernity on numerous counts. Franke offered this characterization in a learning community on "Truth" at the 2005 Emergent Convention in Nashville.

Many see this time of cultural change primarily as a threat to the Christian church. While I believe the growth of the emerging culture requires changes in the church's thinking and practice, I also believe the emerging culture offers a great opportunity for the church to rediscover some of its historical roots and escape some of its contemporary ruts. As we will see, this culture's greater openness and appreciation of mystery can encourage us to embrace our finitude and become more committed to worship an infinite God. It can motivate us to seek God and express the gospel more holistically. We may listen for God's voice in our experiences, with our intuition, through contemplative practices, and from the artistic gifts and experiences of those in our communities. This alone can rescue our view and understanding of God from shallow affirmations and stale—even if they're true—propositions. The emerging culture opens doors of exploration and paths of faithfulness that excite and inspire me. I will make the case that great commitments to community and interdependence can allow us to experience God more fully and to reflect more accurately the character of God within culture and creation.

The emerging culture *will* bring new perils. Any study of the church's journey through history reveals that the dominant cultural perspectives of any era inevitably produce accommodations and contaminations in our understanding and communication of God's character and works. The medieval world shaped a church with mystical superstitions and political entanglements that led to the manipulation and control of an uneducated laity by corrupt elements of the church. The modern world patronized methods of "scientific" biblical interpretation that defanged the Bible of its mystical power and steered our worship toward an overreliance on cognitive study and debate. We should expect challenges similar in weight and threat in the postmodern, emerging culture.

Concerns about the unknown threats the emerging culture may bring for the church can paralyze us. During my more than 20 years of leading cross-cultural international projects with both students and adults, I've always taught that the dangers we face on a daily basis within the comforts of our own culture are often equal to or worse than the dangers of a new environment. Driving a car every day is far more dangerous than the possibility that a black mamba is hidden in a bush and waiting to strike you while you're traveling in Africa.[5] But we fear the new perils *more* because our patterns of anticipation and reflexes of defensiveness against them have, by definition, not formed into habit.

The postmodern culture does pose certain threats and challenges to the gospel, but I believe we've become numb and even casual toward the threats to the gospel that currently exist in our familiar culture. As I hope to demonstrate, in some cases we've codified and blessed some of these threats in the life of the church. For these reasons, I eagerly embrace the church's journey into the emerging culture.

AN EARNEST JOURNEY: THE EMERGING CHURCH

In the midst of this time of cultural transition, a new expression of Christian community is taking shape, one that many call "the emerging church." The emerging church has garnered rising media coverage and public attention in recent years—enough to launch conferences and publishing lines, inspire a growing number of excited devotees, motivate curious leaders seeking to understand its attractions and replicate its model, and galvanize a growing critique and concern.[6] Since it has been my privilege to be a part of these conversations for more than a decade, it's only fair that I share some of my own thoughts and prejudices about the emerging church.

The first question that is typically posed about this new movement surrounds its definition: *What is the emerging church?* While the desire for a definition is understandable, it's the wrong place to start. In many ways the emerging church defies definition. That is part of its allure for some—and its perceived threat for others.

---

[5] The black mamba always represented the most frightening and dangerous creature in our frequent travels to the continent of Africa. Thanks to the many excellent wildlife documentaries on television, the perils of this beautiful and deadly snake were always well-known to the members of our teams, and often took on a mythical quality.

[6] For a recently published and sharply critical perspective, see D.A. Carson's *Becoming Conversant with the Emerging Church* (Grand Rapids, Mich.: Zondervan, 2005).

Andrew Jones is a poet/blogger laureate of the emerging church, and his blog has been a consistent voice of its values and passions. He offered this response when a reader asked him to define the emerging church:

> I have tried to define it and have failed miserably. My apologies. It may be of some console for you to know that no one else has succeeded in defining it, and some of us have been at it a long time. Maybe that is okay. People in the emerging culture do not really want or need such a definition. And some of us are hesitant to give one, because behind the practices and models of emerging church lies a radically different mindset, value system, and worldview.[7]

Andrew's response is wise and in no way evasive. It simply reveals the significant change in perspective that characterizes the emerging culture. The modern world saw definitions as the beginning point for inquiry and understanding. The postmodern world, with its suspicion of universal definitions, rejects this starting point. One can work endlessly to capture the emerging church in a definition and miss the whole point. Nonetheless, Andrew's reply is helpful in getting a sense of the emerging church and its identity.

One reason the emerging church defies definition is because the churches that embrace this label are not monolithic. There are huge diversities in style, organization, theology, and ministry practice among emerging churches. At a recent national conference for the emergent movement, I was in the hotel lounge listening to a conversation among some musicians from an emerging church. Although they appreciated the music at the event, they were quite certain this style of music wouldn't fit well into their own context. And the differences go beyond artistic style. As I've visited various emerging church settings, I've seen a wide range of perspectives on the role of women in the church, reliance on historic theological systems, political leanings, the understanding and practice of the sacraments, church organization, and so much more.

---

[7] Weblog post "Emerging Church Definition 1.0", (February 2, 2004): http://tallskinnykiwi.typepad.com/tallskinnykiwi/2004/02/emerging_church.html

Clearly, the diversity one finds among emerging churches precludes simple generalizations. We should expect that some emerging churches might cross the boundaries of wisdom, propriety, and orthodoxy. We should expect others to find missional paths in the emerging culture that rightfully challenge the ministry trajectory of existing churches. We should also anticipate significant differences among various emerging congregations, as well as areas of surprising continuities with the historic church and more established congregations.

The diversity within the emergent movement also means there is no single model for existing churches to replicate in seeking to transition into emerging culture ministry. Surely existing congregations can learn much from emerging congregations. But there is no single pattern or "system" for a church to follow to minister effectively in our changing culture. Different contexts will require different ministry expressions.

Growing up in North Carolina, I was a huge fan of Coach Dean Smith and his basketball teams at the University of North Carolina. I remember how his familiar nasal twang would bristle in postgame interviews when he was asked about "the Carolina system." His answer was always some version of the following: North Carolina did not have a "system." The players were not locked into some stiff framework that prevented creativity and demanded rote responses to specific game situations. Basketball has far too much complexity for such a method to succeed. Instead, there was a philosophy of play—oriented around principles of effort, unselfishness, and smart decision-making—that was employed creatively within the infinite number of possibilities in any college basketball game.

Coach Smith's retort offers a helpful direction in understanding the emerging church. There is no single model for the theology and practices followed by all emerging churches. But, as Andrew Jones has suggested, the mindsets, values, and perspectives that characterize emerging churches differ from the more systemic and doctrinal approaches of most existing, modern churches.

The emerging church seeks to be an authentic contextualization of the gospel within the values and characteristics of postmodern culture. Therefore, it envisions and expresses Christianity primarily as a way of life, rather than an adherence to a doctrinal system or organizational pattern. This doesn't mean the emerging church is devoid of doctrinal affirmations or structure, but the theological systems or specific ministry models are not the defining factors. Instead, emerging churches are committed to a "rule of life" that includes:

- The pursuit of the gospel expressed and explained in community
- A passion for living out the values of Jesus' kingdom in the present
- Comfort with mystery and uncertainty
- A spiritual holism that calls forth a radical and comprehensive discipleship
- A reading of Scripture that intersects with local stories and contexts
- An experiential approach to both worship and the pursuit of truth
- A ministry that honors the beauty of God's creation and the creative spirit found in humanity[8]

Perhaps most of all, the emerging church is a missional church. By "missional," I mean that the emerging church seeks to be a community that embodies and supports God's mission of establishing a present and future redemptive kingdom.

To a certain extent, this identity is reactive and critical—an alternative to the resource-heavy, needs-based programs of many contemporary churches. But much of the emerging church's identity is creatively generative. It desperately seeks to embody God's agenda in a changing, post-Christian environment where the aging theological constructs and methodologies of a once-dominant religious institution no longer connect as cohesively as they once did.

---

[8] Throughout the following chapters, these characteristics will be fleshed out as I use the passions of the emerging church as a guide for the church's transition.

I must confess I have concerns about the term "emerging church." The "emerging church" label is rapidly becoming the brand name for a popular style of ministry. I talk to many persons who are eager to do "emerging church ministry" without any understanding of the cultural context that breeds the necessity of this ministry or the theological/philosophical developments that inform its practices. Understood in this way, the emerging church can appear to be no more than a new and faddish method divorced from its historical and theological roots.

Discussion about the missional nature of the emerging church can also be offensive to missional Christians from other eras. After a dialogue in our congregation about an emerging church initiative, I was shocked to see a friend and kindred spirit become visibly frustrated. This friend later commented, "'Emerging church' makes it sound like someone just invented these values or cornered the market on creativity." Our church, like many others, has a long history of remarkable creativity, and our efforts to minister effectively in a changing cultural context are not just "emerging" in the present. I concede that this language has its limits and will likely change as the emerging church becomes more established.

As we press forward in this conversation about the church in the emerging culture, I hope two things will be clear. First, I hope you'll see that the emerging church greatly values its relationship with historical expressions of Christianity, both distant and recent. I don't believe—nor does any emergent church leader I know—that the emergent movement has cornered the market on how to embody the gospel creatively in our changing world. But it's also true that God is doing "a new thing" in the ministry and life of the emergent movement. Far more than just a trendy shift in Christian expression, the emerging church embodies a profound and exciting change in understanding God's kingdom and the gospel.

AN INEVITABLE JOURNEY: THE EXISTING CHURCH

As you can see, I have great enthusiasm for the emerging church and its expression of the gospel in the postmodern world. This excitement begs the question of my attitudes, thoughts, and presuppositions related to the existing church.

Church is not a neutral word to me. I bring to any conversation about church a host of personal and professional experiences, a range of prejudices and expectations, and a variety of disappointments and dreams. The church profoundly shaped my childhood. I was blessed to have a wealth of authentic faith and community experiences during my youth; and by the time I was in middle school, I knew I would consider pastoral ministry as a profession. Yet, it's a few moments of intense disappointment with the church I loved that stand out the most in my memory.

Growing up in a rural North Carolina community in the 1960s and 1970s, some of my most painful experiences involved our church community's racism and decisions that were made during the civil rights era. Thanks to the progressive thinking of discerning parents, at an early age I became aware that the Christian community could be disturbingly wrong about cultural issues. I vividly remember my mom's tears when she found out a touring youth choir's visit to our church had been cancelled when our pastor found out the choir had an African-American member. Years later, I learned that my father confronted the pastor over this decision, and some long-time friends in the church never forgave my parents for this confrontation. It remained a source of great pain to my mom right up to the time of her death 10 years later.

By the time I began seminary, I'd had far too many experiences with acts of judgment, fear, ignorance, and isolation—all done in the name of the church and of Christ. At that point, I was studying and training to serve God but not the church. I never expected to work for a church, and I'm certainly not naive about the church's capacity to fail.

But I also have a deep love for the church and a growing optimism about its future. For the past 15 years, I've served as a pastor and elder at the Chapel Hill Bible Church in North Carolina. In this time, I've worked with many people whose spiritual lives have been formed on profound thought, deep compassion, and intense commitment to the gospel Jesus taught and lived. In the culture of this community, materialism has been challenged, hypocrisy avoided, fears confronted, cultural isolation disdained, and graciousness has reigned as a dominant ministry motif. Our congregation is not perfect. Every ministry insider sees the magnitude of human weakness, failure, and sin, as well as the inadequacies of Christian community. Nonetheless, this congregation has wooed me back to a love for the church that was nearly extinguished in my childhood. For this, I will be forever thankful.

The Chapel Hill Bible Church is by no means an emerging church, nor does it seek to become like most emerging churches that have taken shape over the last decade. As a 35-year-old church, our transition into the emerging culture is quite different from fellowships that began with postmodernity as an assumed frame of reference. I don't intend to offer our experiences with navigating the waters of cultural transition as a hardened template for other churches seeking to make the same journey. But our narrative of transition, success, failure, pain, and joy as we've traveled down these waters has influenced every page of this manuscript. The emerging culture conversations within our community have humbled me, helped me understand many of the legitimate fears related to transition, and offered some pathways of generous response to these fears. The willingness of this established church community to hear and dialogue with new thoughts and practices of emerging culture ministry has invigorated my hope for the existing church's ability to transition into this new era.

I believe the existing church is still a viable, needed, and fruitful expression of Christian community in our culture. In other words, I don't think the existing church is a candidate for reformation by extermination. I don't hope for the demise of the existing church.

Like many of Christ's followers, I have many frustrations with the existing church. When I watch certain late-night religious broadcasts, I feel like an uninvited and unwelcome intruder at the scene of an automobile accident. I struggled during the U.S. presidential election of 2004 when the polarities of the Christian community seemed to match our nation's political divisions. I sometimes wonder whether the most politically organized segments of the church have read the whole Bible or just a few prooftexts that affirm their politics.[9] I cringe when the church insists on practicing any of a variety of cultural anachronisms, baptizing these practices with divine affirmation and thus diminishing the voice of the church in a constantly changing world.

But, inevitably, the moment I lapse into a state of religious self-righteousness and arrogant confidence that proclaims I know something that you don't but should, I'm surprised and appropriately shamed by the depth and quality of the existing church. I am shamed when persons with whom I regularly disagree far exceed my ability or desire to express Christian love in certain situations. I am shamed when these brothers and sisters express care for me even though we don't see eye-to-eye theologically. (Would I have done so had the roles been reversed?) I am constantly surprised and humbled by the creativity, passion, and effectiveness I witness in churches that are not on the cutting edge of the emerging culture conversation.

The existing church continues to serve faithfully the mission and message of Christ in this in-between world of intermingled modern and postmodern cultures. Though I will say much about this emerging culture's demands for transition in the existing church, I never want to lose sight of this assumption.

I also believe that although the church has a natural aversion to change, it also has a long history of effective adaptation to cultural transition. I believe this will continue to be true for the existing church as it confronts the emerging culture.

[9]Even before I read it, I knew I'd love Jim Wallis's book, *God's Politics: Why the Right Gets It Wrong and the Left Doesn't Get It* (San Francisco: HarperSanFrancisco, 2005)!

My brother-in-law, Tony Martin, has been a worship pastor in Southern Baptist churches for his whole professional career. Immediately after his graduation from Davidson College, he took a worship ministry position in a small, rural church in North Carolina. He likes to tell how he enthusiastically bounded into the choir room for his first rehearsal and noticed the rather small choir of primarily senior citizens was scattered throughout the room. He urged the choir members to sit closer together so they could hear one another's voices. This suggestion prompted many protests: "No, that's Robert's chair," or "I could never take Nancy's chair." Encouraged by the prospect of a much larger choir, Tony beamed and exclaimed, "I can't wait to meet all these folks! Do you think they'll be here next week?" Sadly, the remaining choir members then explained that Robert, Nancy, and all the other owners of those vacant chairs had "passed on to their reward with the Lord."

This is the image many people have of the church—a collection of dear but inflexible people who save chairs for dead people. For years, I attended emerging church gatherings where little hope was expressed for the existing church. And as we look at the memorial plaques and stained-glass windows of historic church buildings or hear outdated practices justified by an omnipresent "that's just the way we do things here," it's easy to assume the church never changes. But I sense this tone changing for two reasons.

First, even a cursory study of church history reveals that the church eventually adapts to cultural change. This change can be frighteningly slow and with many embarrassments along the way—see the flat earth theory, monkey trials, and support of slavery for evidence. Nevertheless, the unique blessing of the presence of God's Spirit in the church assures eventual changes in the direction of God's mission. The church has crossed great divides such as the Jewish/Gentile debate in the early church and the frightening challenges of the Renaissance and scientific revolution. It will also respond to the challenges of our changing cultural context.

Secondly, the emerging culture is already having a profound impact on the existing church. Some measure of transition has begun. The surface evidence includes the growing number of emerging church plants supported by established churches and denominations, the development of alternative services in more traditional churches, and the major media attention directed toward these ministries.[10] But, as I will argue throughout this book, real transition involves more than stylistic change. The greater evidence of transition lies in a new language and conceptualization of ministry in existing churches that runs far deeper than "postmodern" worship services, video cafés, and marketing pieces with "old-school" monastic fonts.

Our church in Chapel Hill offers an example. Being in a university community, our default for spiritual nurture is cognitive, teaching programs. When in doubt, we've traditionally created a classroom experience. As we've stated, the emerging culture has contributed to a rising interest in experiential spirituality, spiritual holism, and the spiritual practices of historic Christianity. These interests have greatly impacted our nomenclature and programmatic design for spiritual development. Contemplative prayer retreats have become common. Requests for spiritual direction or spiritual directors fill my inbox. And contemplative experiences, such as the Stations of the Cross, now find their way onto our church calendar.

Our emerging culture ministry initiative began with a significant group of "Bible churchers" gathering in my living room at sunrise to pray a morning, liturgical office. We now speak of "spiritual formation"—a term that embraces emerging culture understandings of holism and experience in spiritual growth—rather than "discipleship" (a wonderful term that has been associated with cognitive-only approaches, at least in our tradition). I like to needle a colleague whose job title now includes "spiritual formation," a phrase that used to make him nervous and uncomfortable because it seemed a bit "liberal" and "vague"![11]

---

[10] Although there has been much coverage of the emerging church in major newspapers, network specials, online pieces, and in national periodicals, so far the majority of the coverage has focused on stylistic features like music, worship service design, or the cultural stereotypes of those who attend these ministries.

[11] One example of this in conservative Christian fellowships (many of which may have concerns about the emerging culture and church) would be the intense support of Mel Gibson's film *The Passion of the Christ*. This film was deeply influenced by the Stations of the Cross—an ancient Catholic representation of Jesus' final hours that has been the source for many historical and contemplative prayer experiences, as well as the inspiration of so much art.

I can think of scores of friends who were defensively locked in doctrinal and cultural-avoidance expressions of Christianity in the mid-1990s, but are now eagerly devouring emergent books. One of these friends recently approached me with a copy of Brian McLaren's *A Generous Orthodoxy* under his arm. He pointed to the book and said, "This is the kind of Christianity I want to follow and lead." My dropping jaw prevented even a pithy reply of, "I told you so!" There is little doubt that a transition in the existing church has begun.

This transition is both inevitable and necessary. For the church to thrive in the emerging culture of the present and future, it must embark on this journey. The church will increasingly find that some of its theological conceptions are founded on philosophical premises and cultural conditions that will be deeply marginalized in the future—if they exist at all. As a result, some of the traditional divisions of the church, modes of theological communication, and ministry forms will wane in significance and impact. This doesn't mean an end to our traditions. (I'll take up the fear of losing our traditions later.) But it does mean change lies ahead. For the church to maintain its voice in the emerging culture, transition is necessary.

TRANSITION: A JOURNEY OF MANY PATHS

Although transition is essential, the church's journey into the emerging culture will follow no single path, nor will each congregation arrive at the same destination. The existing church's journey of transition will take many forms and will embrace a variety of goals. While we'll explore the nature of the necessary transitions throughout the book, a few broad areas bear mentioning now.

First, while the church as a whole must transition, not every congregation will or should pursue these new directions. Some churches need to continue in their current paradigm of ministry, either because it has proven successful in their particular context or because the costs of transition are too high at the moment. The consequences of cultural disconnect for those who ignore or resist the emerging culture will be very real and in some cases increasingly painful. We must recognize that emerging culture transition cannot occur through a midnight takeover of a local congregation that leaves faithful followers lost in a new environment without a working language, compass bearings, or meaningful symbols. The pace of transition should vary widely between churches. Transition to emerging culture ministries will be much easier, more natural, and far more necessary in some communities than others. And some methods and practices will not translate to every community. But along with the opportunities, there will be unexpected costs and casualties in every situation.

Second, I want to stress that I'm not suggesting that the existing churches' goal of transition is to replicate the forms of current emerging churches. Many emerging churches are the product of church-planting endeavors that offer far more freedom and a radically different context than that which faces existing churches. To try to blindly copy these communities—rather than seeking to learn from their passions and organizing principles—is an act of reckless naiveté.

The form that existing churches will take as they transition into the emerging culture is still significantly unknown. Nevertheless, the existing church can learn much from emerging churches, despite their radically divergent contexts. The emerging church can play a prophetic role for established churches, charting the path into new territory. Although the emergent movement did not begin with this goal, this opportunity to guide the existing church into new lands presents itself as a great potential blessing for the emerging church.

Conversely, existing churches have an opportunity to serve as both student and mentor to the emerging church. The emerging church doesn't need to develop in isolation. Instead, the existing church can play a critical role in shaping the future of the emerging church. With the support and blessing of existing churches, the emerging church can diversify, mature, and avoid some of the mistakes existing churches have made.

Unfortunately, there are already more than enough examples of emerging churches that feel they have cornered the market on creativity or invented the concept of cultural authenticity. At the same time, existing churches have often been far too quick to offer harsh critiques of emerging churches based on their expectations of "success" and theological correctness. Nonetheless, there remains a great opportunity for mutual blessing and partnership between the existing church and the emerging church.

Tyler Jones is the founding pastor of Vintage21, an emerging church with a blossoming ministry in Raleigh, North Carolina. A gifted, former staff member of a campus ministry, Tyler has often stated how much he appreciates having an opportunity to "talk shop" with leaders from established churches with a far longer history than his own fellowship. As I've traveled and networked in the emergent community, I constantly find this attitude among both younger and older leaders in the emerging church.

The results of the collaboration between existing and emerging churches can be quite special. Many existing congregations have thrived amidst cultural changes that have demanded huge risks and startling creativity. And, of course, there is no substitute for experience. While there may be huge differences in the worship gatherings, thought patterns, and goals between existing and emerging churches, there are certainly realities of "church" that transcend these differences.

Recently, I was interviewing leaders in emerging church settings about ministry models that involved church collaboration with entrepreneurial businesses. The emerging church's desire to partner with the business world stands in marked contrast to the more compartmentalized modern culture, which has sought to maintain a firewall between the business world and the church community. While our congregation has been heavily shaped by the modern compartmentalization of church and business, we are also located in a university town. Thus, we've experienced numerous occasions where a professor in our fellowship has taken some research or creation to the market, often employing others in our church community in the process. Some of these ventures have succeeded; others have failed, leading to job loss and potential brokenness in our fellowship. Through careful communication, reconciliation, and pastoral care, our congregation has navigated and survived the perilous waters of failed business ventures and even the jealousy of successful businesses. This is just one example of how the emergent church might learn from the storehouse of experiences of the existing church, even in areas where there might be significant differences of philosophy and practice.

Finally, let me close this chapter with a word about the relationship between theology and methodology in the emerging culture ministry. There are many who'd like to think the existing church's transition into effective ministry in the emerging culture will involve nothing more than the utilization of some creative, new worship styles and ministry methods. As I will stress throughout the book, I firmly believe the church's authentic journey into the emerging culture must involve transitions in both thought and practice.

I had a balding university professor who would part what little hair he had just above one ear and comb it over the top to create the illusion of a full head of hair. When he would bend over the podium, his large lecture classes would inevitably simmer in snickers and chuckles as his "secret hair restoration method" was revealed. He was simply a bald guy pretending to have a full head of hair. Churches that seek to copy the practices and methods of emerging church ministry without simultaneously pursuing the dialogue of transition in thought are very likely to exhibit the inauthenticity of a really bad comb-over. The practices do not make sense without the theology.

The relationship of thought to practice in the emerging culture is reciprocal. The thought and practice inform each other; each can look quite foolish alone.[12] This obvious and essential point is so often lost in our driving pragmatism to embrace—or reject—new methods. I will come back to this point again and again as we examine the theological dialogues and practices of transition. This is, without a doubt, one principle of transition that must not be ignored or forgotten.

With that said, we turn now to thought and theological issues that are foundational and instrumental to church transition. Our lens in examining these matters is a series of fears that can derail essential dialogues of theological transition.

---

[12] This is true for the relationship of thought to practice in every era. The practices of worship and spiritual nurture for the modern church were formed and informed by the epistemology and philosophy of the Enlightenment and the modern era.

CHAPTER TWO

Seven Deadly Fears and Seven Essential Conversations, Part 1: Culture and the Gospel

I'd just finished leading a dialogue on churches in transition, when a friend spoke up with a bit of a confession. "I really came to discuss the new model of 'doing church,'" he explained. "But now I see this conversation also requires an examination of our theology. The theology and the practices go hand in hand."

My friend is right on target. Theological exploration is often a route to greater conviction, liberation, and changes in practice or behavior. Much of what I do in pastoral counseling and spiritual direction involves theological dialogue. Often, these sessions lead to new or expanded understandings of God's identity and purposes—understandings that liberate us from shame, guilt, patterns of painful behavior, or spiritual stagnation.

Theological questions can also involve tremendous fears. In my seminary days, a favored colloquialism of both professors and students was the mythical "slippery slope." The clear implication was that there were lines of theological inquiry that, even if gently pursued, could result in a treacherous or even fatal plummet. The slippery slope warning was like the governor on an engine, intended to keep our theological inquiry at safe speeds and on firm, level ground.

This penchant for extreme caution in wrestling with theological questions has been well learned in most Christian communities. The result is that the kind of theological exploration the church needs as it transitions into a new culture is often impeded by fear and hijacked by oversimplifications inspired by those fears.

When our church was just beginning an emerging culture ministry initiative, I preached a series of sermons on the theological issues, lessons, and practices that I felt were enhanced by emerging culture sensitivities. In my first sermon, I spoke about how the grand narrative of God's redemptive story could transcend and even redeem the pain of our personal stories without the burden of explaining our pain. The next morning, I ran into a volunteer who was using the copier in our church office. She told me she'd found a great deal of hope in the sermon. She'd been through a series of tormenting events in her life, but the sermon offered her a profound experience of freedom.

I went straight from this conversation to my computer, where I found an e-mail written to our entire board of elders. The subject line said, "Emerging Church Initiative—Tim Conder Sermon." It clearly was not an affirmation note! The lengthy letter that followed was not from an angry, immature, or anonymous person. It came from a mature and sensible Christian with whom I'd had a long relationship. The letter declared the emerging church to be "liberal psycho-babble" and "useless as the basis for mission" in a church like ours. The letter's final words were uncompromising: "In conclusion, my feeling is that at best the emerging church is a troubling disruption that detracts from the main tasks of the church; at worst, it's a heretical movement that provides Satan a tool to delude the saints."

That which is deeply liberating for some can seem frightening or heretical to others. While one church member found a word of life in my sermon, another's reaction seemed rooted in oversimplified fears of liberal theology, the slippery slope of heresy, and satanic influence.

Fears of this magnitude not only prevent theological dialogue, they also create experiences of isolation and invalidation. A graduate student in our community experiences the pain and frustration of having her vibrant but thoroughly postmodern faith devalued by those she loves. Every time she returns to the church of her youth, they lovingly label her as a heretic and constantly try to "convert" her to the faith she has already chosen. We chatted one morning after church and she commented, "You know, it's Sunday morning—they're probably praying for my salvation right now!" She feels tremendously displaced and devalued in the existing church. Her questions, thoughts, and perspectives are labeled as dangerous—or at least unwelcome.

The theological and ethical questions that emerging culture interests raise for the church are often caricatured and oversimplified in ways that prevent fruitful dialogue. The loser in this scenario is the church. So many pastors tell me they feel they're being held hostage by strong fears in their congregations. We live in a world where modern and postmodern perspectives not only collide in the media, in political loyalties, and in culture wars, but also sit side by side in the pews of our churches. Many pastors in the existing church feel like baseball pitchers. They're standing alone on the mound, looking in at the catcher, and seeing not one, but two different home plates. There's no way to throw a pitch that will cross both plates for a strike. So these pastors feel doomed to throw a "ball" to at least one batter on every pitch. Worst of all, in many congregations there is a fear-filled silence that prevents any open discussion of this dilemma.

In this chapter, and the two that follow, we'll examine seven fear-inspired over-simplifications that often infect the existing church when we think about ministry in the emerging culture. I call them the "Seven Deadly Fears" because if they're not confronted, these fears can prevent theological dialogue, impede the church's ability to consider the issues of emerging culture transition, and even mitigate the potential blessings the church can receive from questions raised in the emerging culture.[13]

But there is hope, if we're willing to open the closet and examine these fears. For buried behind each one of them is a conversation the church needs to have as it considers the path of transition into the emerging culture.

The first three fears are concerns related to the identity of the gospel and its interaction with culture:

- Postmodernism and the loss of "truth"
- Community and the loss of "personal faith"
- Cultural "accommodation" and changing the "changeless" message of the gospel

---

[13] In our church these fears have been the dominant points of concern (and conversation stoppers in some settings) as we've envisioned ministry in the emerging culture. These seven may parallel issues being raised by some scholars as well, but they are offered here in the "voice" of the church.

My hope in addressing these fears is to move the conversation from these dead-end streets to dialogues that include paths of rich possibility for the future of the church.

POSTMODERNISM AND THE LOSS OF "TRUTH"

The first deadly fear: The emerging culture's attachment to postmodern thought leaves no room for the truth of the gospel.

Postmodernism has become the ultimate red herring in conversations between many existing churches and those doing ministry in the emerging culture. While postmodern thinking has shaped the emerging culture and many emerging churches, many in the existing church believe a postmodern understanding is antithetical to the gospel.

I became aware of the significance of postmodernism for the church in October 1993, when I was asked to join a small think tank on the topic of ministry to Generation X. At that time, the news and entertainment industries were making the term "Gen-X" inescapable, and this generational analysis of our culture was front and center in many new models of ministry. At this gathering, theologian Stan Grenz made a persuasive presentation about the importance of postmodernism in understanding our shifting culture.[14] For me, this was a moment of revelation, a time when "the lights came on" and I began to realize the significance this philosophical shift had for Christian ministry.

Grenz suggests that postmodernism represents a rejection or deconstruction of the modern, Enlightenment worldview. This deconstruction includes a disbelief in the goodness of knowledge, the certainty and rational nature of truth, and the objectivity of knowledge (separate from human experiences).[15]

From these three points of rejection, one can see some of the passions of postmodern culture: an emphasis on beauty (since knowledge is not inherently good), holism (since truth cannot be

---

[14] This consortium produced several significant books, including Stanley Grenz's *A Primer on Postmodernism* (Grand Rapids, Mich.: Wm. B. Eerdmans, 1996) and Jimmy Long's *Generating Hope* (Downers Grove, Ill.: InterVarsity Press, 1997).

[15] Stanley Grenz offers this "early" definition of postmodernism particularly to Christian readers in *A Primer on Postmodernism* (Grand Rapids, Mich.: Wm. B. Eerdmans, 1996), 2, 7-8.

ascertained by cognitive inquiry alone), and community (since knowledge must be derived from a variety of contexts, perspectives, and experiences). Whether in art, literature, film, ethics, politics, theology, or simply in the association of friends, postmodernism is often associated or equated with a mood or ethos of pessimism (even nihilism), uncertainty, subjective and situational understandings of morality, and local or contextual understandings of truth.

Given these characteristics, it's not surprising that postmodernism has provoked great fear and strong critiques from many in the Christian community. You've probably heard these critiques before—that postmodern people do not believe in God, truth, or reality.[16] The same criticisms are levied at the emerging church, due to its association with a postmodern worldview. In many ways, we in the emerging church movement have set ourselves up for this backlash due to our unabashed and uncritical enthusiasm for all things postmodern. We've let postmodernism become the lazy and convenient straw man for emerging church critics and the undefined mascot for emerging church enthusiasts.

For many who might otherwise learn much from the emerging church, the key issue is a fear of the loss of truth (and hope) in our theology. Christians are united in their passionate belief in the truth of the Christian faith and the hope it offers to humanity. In many minds, postmodernism represents the absence of absolute truth and eternal hope. But those who leap to this understanding must realize there are many different strands of postmodernism, as well as a wide variety of theologies associated with postmodernism.[17]

Philosopher Nancey Murphy of Fuller Theological Seminary has written persuasively about the fundamental differences between Anglo-American postmodernity and the European (or continental) postmodernity so often linked to nihilism, atheism, and the denial of truth.[18] Brian McLaren—pastor, author, and emerging church leader—has humorously and accurately challenged the notion that the postmodern theology of the emerging church is simply a philosophical disguise for disbelief in ultimate truths and realities. In

---

[16] One of the more humorous critiques comes from Chuck Colson, "The Postmodern Crack-Up: From soccer moms to college campuses, signs of the end," *Christianity Today*, December 2003.

[17] Stanley Grenz and John Franke, in *Beyond Foundationalism* (Louisville, Ky.: Westminster John Knox Press, 2001), describe the diversity and numerous strands in postmodern theology, drawing on the work of Kevin J. Vanhoozer.

[18] See Nancey Murphy in *Anglo-American Postmodernity* (Boulder, Colo.: Westview Press, 1997).

response to an editorial from Chuck Colson in *Christianity Today*, McLaren writes,

> What you describe as postmodernism—a claim that "there is no such thing as truth," a rejection of all moral values, or their reduction to mere preferences—may have been purported by a few crazed graduate students for a few minutes at a late-night drinking party. But to paint the whole movement with that brush is inaccurate.[19]

Theologians Stan Grenz and John Franke have stressed the positive possibilities and contributions postmodernism is making to current theological thought:

> Clearly postmodernism cannot be dismissed as nothing more than a deconstructive agenda that stands in stark opposition to Christian faith and thought. On the contrary, there is much evidence that suggests that the postmodern context has actually been responsible for the renewal of theology as an intellectual discipline after a period of stagnation.[20]

Postmodernism can neither be collapsed into a single all-encompassing definition nor dismissed with a single critique. But as I often remind the members of our church, postmodernism is not the point! Our goal is not to be a postmodern church or to affirm postmodernism any more than our goal is to reject any and all things associated with this worldview. Our goal is to embody the gospel of Jesus Christ authentically as a community in an ever-changing culture. For the church to be effective and authentic in this day, we must better understand postmodernity, become conversant with postmodern people, and be able to function in the midst of many postmodern assumptions.

Although I cannot predict the future scope of postmodernism, there is little doubt that postmodernity plays a significant role in our emerging culture. If the existing church is going to enter the

---

[19] Brian McLaren, "An open letter to Chuck Colson", posted on *anewkindofchristian.com/archives/000269. html*. In this letter, Brian described seven potential meanings for the word "truth" that help to widen this conversation beyond harsh generalizations.

[20] Grenz and Franke, 22.

emerging culture, we must stop equating emerging culture with our worst fears about postmodernity.

Invitation to Conversation: Philosophical Reflection

I believe the emerging church's association—even its infatuation—with postmodern thinking offers the existing church an invitation into greater authenticity through dialogue and philosophical reflection.

Many portions of the church are resistant to utilizing philosophical study and reflection as tools for understanding the gospel and expanding our worship and witness. The early church father Tertullian's question, "What has Athens to do with Jerusalem?" lives on in many congregations.[21] Yet the church also has a long history of philosophical inquiry. When the early church wrestled with the huge theological questions related to the deity and humanity of Christ and the perplexing reality of the Trinity, it leaned heavily on the philosophical thinking of its day.[22] The leaders of the early church used the philosophy of that era not only to communicate the gospel to their culture but also to clarify their own understanding of the Scriptures and Christian faith.

Theological historian Roger Olson describes how Greek philosophy shaped early Christian efforts in teaching and evangelism:

> The second-century Christian apologists chose instead to defend the truth of Christianity on the basis of the philosophies of Platonism and Stoicism...they found much common ground between the Christian life and worldview and the generic blend of Platonism and Stoicism that made up the common Greek philosophy of much of the Roman empire in the second century...Greek philosophy was monotheistic rather than polytheistic and contended strongly for the ultimately spiritual nature of the reality behind and beneath the visible things. It also affirmed the immortality of souls and the importance of living a good life of ethical behavior that sought the balance between extremes and avoided pure sensuality and selfishness.[23]

[21] Roger Olson, *The Story of Christian Theology* (Downers Grove, Ill.: InterVarsity Press, 1999), 84.

[22] Olson, 180. See chapter five in this volume for a more detailed narrative about the interplay between philosophy and theology in the early church.

[23] Olson, 55-57.

Greek philosophy also served as a critical tool for teaching the Christian faith in the midst of heresies. Olson explains how Clement of Alexandria, in the late second and early third centuries, supported philosophical reflection to enhance Christian theological understanding:

> Clement believed philosophy could aid in Christianity's fight against heresies. False teachings often arise from mental confusion; philosophy tries to be logical and uses dialectic (critical examination) to test true claims and beliefs. If God's revelation is intelligible, then using logic and dialectic to study interpretations of it will surely lead to a sounder set of beliefs and morals than ignoring them.[24]

Philosophical reflection and inquiry were essential in the development of the thinking of early church leaders. The emerging church's exploration of postmodernism (with its associated critique of Enlightenment assumptions such as empiricism) is helping to restore this asset to the church.

As the existing church dialogues with the emerging church and journeys into the emerging culture, the essential conversation is not about postmodernism (and especially our generalized fears about postmodernism). Our focus should be on the quality of our philosophical reflection. Can philosophy be one of many tools that inform our theology and practices? Can our philosophical analysis offer insight on our humanity, the nature of God, the presence of God's redemption in our lives and communities, and the hope of the gospel? When does philosophy become an end in itself and the foolish "wisdom of the world" of which Paul warns us in 1 Corinthians 1:18–2:5? These are the questions that should shape our conversations.

The philosophical reflections prompted by the emerging culture can sharpen our understanding of God's redemptive presence in our lives and in our communion with God. Postmodernism's penchant for uncertainty and the emerging church's willingness to

---

[24] Olson, 88.

incorporate uncertainty into its thinking produce a higher awareness of the mystery of God. This renewed understanding of mystery is invigorating a sense of awe and exploration in the worship of many churches. It has become safe again to say, "I don't know," and to allow the sense of human finitude to draw our worshipful attention toward an infinite God.

The postmodern sensitivity to the importance of community is expanding our understanding of God's redemptive work. Shaped by the individualism of the Enlightenment, church teaching regarding salvation and redemption has focused almost entirely on the personal and individual—particularly individual freedom from guilt. But now we also teach about the social dimension of salvation in our liberation from shame.[25] This is a gospel that many in our world need to hear.

The emphasis on community has also catalyzed *local* expressions of mission. Particularly in conservative churches, there has been great emphasis on international evangelism in mission. But many congregations now see ministries of compassion and evangelism in their local communities as central expressions of mission. This is further evidence of the sensitivities of the emerging, postmodern culture affecting the church.

Philosophical reflection is a historic practice of the church that, when restored to prominence, can bear great fruit for our congregational life. Many emerging churches have begun this journey and would welcome the collaboration and partnership of more established churches along the way. When we can get beyond our oversimplifications, accusations, and fears, the church's honest and faithful engagement with postmodern philosophical thought can deepen its theology and enliven its mission.

---

[25] Shame is an experience we have in community. In Genesis 2:25, the first man and woman are depicted living in harmony. In Genesis 2:7-10, the first experience of the man and woman in the wake of their sins was shame and fear. See *Generating Hope* (Downers Grove, Ill.: InterVarsity Press, 1997), by Jimmy Long, for a good explanation of the social dimensions of salvation.

COMMUNITY AND THE LOSS OF "PERSONAL FAITH"

The second deadly fear: The emerging culture's emphasis on community minimizes the importance of personal faith.

Individualism has dominated the American identity. In his defining study on U.S. culture, *Habits of the Heart*, sociologist Robert Bellah describes our individualism in these strong terms:

> Individualism lies at the very core of American culture...We believe in the dignity, indeed the sacredness, of the individual. Anything that would violate our right to think for ourselves, judge for ourselves, make our own decisions, live our lives as we see fit, is not only morally wrong, it's sacrilegious. Our highest and noblest aspirations, not only for ourselves, but for those we care about, for our society and for the world, are closely linked to our individualism.[26]

No wonder so many Christians talk about God's redemptive work almost exclusively in individual and personal terms. Describing our faith, we often utilize language like "my Savior," "my times with the Lord," "my worship," and "my personal relationship with God." I sometimes jest that such speech makes Jesus sound like a personal banker.

Emerging culture notions of community bring a strong rebuttal to this individualism. Those of us who are sensitive to this critique have begun to teach, preach, and even plead about the importance of community, perhaps to extremes. This emphasis leads to fears that community is the real god of the emerging culture, and that emerging culture ministry no longer affirms personal faith and communion with God.

At the strong risk of confirming such fears, I would like to raise the question: Was there ever really a "personal faith" in the first place? Let me explain. In a recent Sunday class, a dear friend expressed concern that my talk of community seemed to ignore the

---

[26] Robert Bellah, *Habits of the Heart* (Berkeley, Calif.: Univ. of California Press, 1985), 142.

47

value of personal faith. I asked him to give an example of personal faith. He responded by telling of his times of personal prayer and communion with God, long hikes for the purpose of prayer, private times of prayer in the morning, and extended silent retreats. While all of these are great examples of a mature spiritual life, I would contend that they are, in fact, acts of community rather than personal faith.

Who taught us to pray? Our prayers are never isolated acts and experiences crafted by the one who prays. We pray to a triune God who pursued us first. When we pray, our words are often drawn from Scripture, the historical church, or memorized prayers shared with us by loving parents or friends (truly some of the best liturgies!). When we pray, we join a community of persons all over the world who also seek communion with God. The same is true of reading the Bible. In Scripture, we are reading stories once shared orally around a campfire. We are reading the experiences of communities that struggled with God's leading and plans. We are reading inspired words penned by a diverse community of persons, and then interpreted by the Israelites and the church for thousands of years. When we fear the loss of "personal faith," I wonder if we are defending a concept that never existed.

This is not to say there is no sense of the individual in the Bible and in Christian tradition. The value of the individual is critical to Christian theology. Our faith doesn't envision a future state when individuals evaporate or disappear into nothingness. We teach that each and every human being was created uniquely in the image of God (Genesis 9:6). In the poetry of Psalm 139, God's intimate knowledge of every person is beautifully described:

> O Lord, you have searched me and you know me. You know when I sit and when I rise; you perceive my thoughts from afar. You discern my going out and my lying down; you are familiar with all my ways. Before a word is on my tongue you know it completely, O Lord. You hem me in—behind and before; you have laid your hand upon me. (Psalm 139:1-5)

To the thief who was crucified with Jesus and who reached out in faith, Jesus promised personal salvation (Luke 23:43). In 1 Corinthians 15, the apostle Paul teaches of a future when individuals will experience resurrection like that of Christ. Surely, our faith has relevance to each of us as individuals.

But all of this profound and hopeful biblical individualism comes in the context of community. The narrative of the Scriptures describes God's work of redemption coming through communities of worshippers. God took Abraham and formed a nation, a community of hope for the entire world (Genesis 12:1-3). Jesus formed an intimate and diverse community that became the relational center of his ministry on earth. This same community was transformed into the church after his death and resurrection. Even our most precious teaching about individuals—the assurance that each of us can experience an intimate relationship with God—is a mysterious and gracious act of community.

As C.S. Lewis wrote in his classic text, *Mere Christianity*, the Christian faith is not about the personal affirmation of a belief system. Instead, it is entry into a relationship in which we are joined mysteriously by God's Spirit into the "three-personed," triune community life of God.[27] The defense of personal faith can be a fearful argument that leads away from these spiritual realities.

Invitation to Conversation: Biblical Community Versus Community as Cultural Idol

As the church interacts with the emerging culture, the more critical question is: How can we embody true biblical community in a culture that idolizes community yet sees too few authentic expressions of it?

Community is one of the most overused and misused words in our current vocabulary. The term is employed wistfully and romantically as the ultimate goal, need, and destination of all persons. But what we often call "community" is often very far from authentic community. Bellah explains that true communities are diverse, in-

---

27 C.S. Lewis, *Mere Christianity* (New York: Macmillan Company, 1952), 142,153.

49

terdependent, and involve both public and private aspects of life. In other words, community is challenging, cross-cultural, pervasive, and sometimes messy. Rather than engaging in the difficult work of pursuing true community, we're willing to accept false "communities" founded on similarity and lifestyle. Bellah calls these associations "lifestyle enclaves" and distinguishes them from authentic community:

> Whereas a community attempts to be an inclusive whole, celebrating the interdependence of public and private life and of the different callings of all, lifestyle is fundamentally segmental and celebrates the narcissism of similarity.[28]

Much of what passes for community in contemporary culture is simply a social extension of individualism. We establish community groups that are icons of personal fulfillment, affirmations of consumerism and personal tastes, and bastions of homogeneity. Many of our neighborhoods and suburban subdivisions, social clubs, recreational gatherings, and sadly our churches might be more appropriately called lifestyle enclaves rather than community. Bellah noted that even religious and political groups drawn together by a shared commitment to certain ideals struggled with this dynamic. Writing about his studies of both conservative evangelicals and liberal community activists, he concludes:

> To the extent that their serious commitments carry them beyond private life into public endeavors, they do indeed transcend the lifestyle enclave and represent genuine community. But the tendency of contemporary American life is to pull all of us into lifestyle enclaves of one sort or another.[29]

Bellah's words energize the questions about individualism and community that frame the essential dialogue for the church as it enters the emerging culture. Will the church form authentic communities? Will today's Christian church reflect God's work of re-

---

[28] Bellah, 72.
[29] Bellah, 74.

demptive community formation as seen throughout the biblical narrative? How will we respond to and, in many ways, resist the trend of community formation that has become a cultural expectation and icon?

Let's not waste energy defending personal faith from the encroaching idol of community. Instead, let's talk about the nature and expression of authentic biblical community as a gateway for the church's transition into the emerging culture.

CULTURAL "ACCOMMODATION" AND CHANGING THE "CHANGELESS" MESSAGE OF THE GOSPEL

The third deadly fear: Attempts to do culturally relevant ministry in an emerging culture cause the gospel message to be softened and distorted.

"We're letting culture into the church! We're watering down and altering the gospel with the mindset of our culture!" Like nearly every other pastor I know, I've heard these voices of alarm in the face of a decision or new direction. Sometimes I've been the one expressing the concern (again, like most pastors I know).

In the mid-1980s, I was a strong critic of the predominance of corporate language, methods, and expectations in ministry decisions and programs. I was uncomfortable with how corporate leadership paradigms, language of "measurable goals and returns," and expectations of "excellence" within ministry were shaping the gospel message and the life of our church. More recently, I've been the one defending the use of new technologies and contemporary cultural idioms—as well as historic idioms that predate the comfort of our fellowship—in the life and worship of the church. I've encouraged our use of monastic paradigms, the language of spiritual holism, expectations of uncertainty, and diverse artistic expression within the church. Clearly, I've been on both sides of this question of how culture shapes our expression of the gospel.

I believe we need to be sensitive to inappropriate cultural intrusion in our method and message. We must ask whether our use of cultural material is prejudicial or hypocritical (arbitrarily favoring some cultural material over others).[30] But we need to recognize that the message and practice of the church has never been—nor will it ever be—culture-free. Thank goodness! The presence of human culture in the gospel makes it unique, liberating, and believable. "Cultural intrusion" is one of the hallmarks of Christian thought, belief, and history. We worship a God who chose to be revealed in the historical texts we call Scripture. These texts were written by human authors using the cultural idioms, metaphors, and language of their day. We call these texts the "Word of God" and often "the gospel."

We also teach that God is revealed in the person of Jesus Christ. God took on the frailties, inadequacies, and finitude not only of human flesh, but also of a particular culture and time (Philippians 2:5-11). Jesus ate the local food and spoke the local language. He sang the people's songs and danced their dances. He used the thought forms and expectations of the culture to shape his stories and to inspire his pictures of the eternal kingdom of heaven that he promised. And Jesus, too, was called the "Word of God" (John 1:1-14). The basis and uniqueness of our faith is an incarnate Word and an incarnate God—both graciously intrusive in human history and intruded upon not only by the human cultures of their day, but also by every human culture that seeks to interpret the Scriptures.

At a recent church meeting, one of our church leaders commented that talk about our emerging culture ministry sounded a lot like what she hears at the education vision meetings she regularly attends as a school principal. "The curriculum never changes," she said, "but our methodology for presenting this curriculum must be constantly adapting. The emerging culture requires new methodology for a timeless gospel."

Her comment represents a fairly common summary—and I'm sure it was intended to be supportive. But I don't quite agree with it.

---

[30] This happens regularly when we arbitrarily assign sacred value to a particular cultural era or mode of expression. In the common conflict over music in some churches, hymns have been justified inappropriately as more sacred than contemporary musical forms. In reality, our traditional hymns were deeply influenced by the tunes and music of popular culture. Arguments of musical quality, theological honesty and accuracy, accessibility, and many other points of evaluation are far better talking points in these discussions.

I believe that in the context of the emerging culture, as in any other culture, the message has changed and is continuously changing. What's more, I believe this should be cause for excitement rather than alarm.

As we've said, there has never been a culture-free gospel. The message of the gospel has always been shaped by the interests, worldview, prejudices, and communicational mediums of the culture in which it is being communicated. In pre-literary times, when the gospel was primarily spoken rather than written, the message faced challenges of inappropriate embellishment by personal nuances and interests of the speaker. In a mass-media based culture, the gospel is sometimes reduced to memorable sound bites. The body of teaching we call the gospel—the teachings of Jesus and the narrative of Scripture—is constantly being embellished and reinterpreted as it encounters new eras and methods of communication. While we must be wary of the ways the message can be reduced or distorted by cultural intrusion, changing cultural realities also offer tremendous opportunity for new and deepened understandings to emerge.

I realize the idea of the gospel as a changing message is difficult for many to swallow. I recall teaching a class on the emerging culture to a group of older adults in our fellowship. Their years of faithfulness to the gospel far exceeded my own meager efforts. One woman with many decades of cross-cultural ministry experience politely bristled at my assertion that there is no such thing as a culture-free gospel: "Can you give even one example of how culture has infiltrated the gospel message in the recent evangelical tradition?" I gently responded that our church sits in a community that was racially segregated not many years ago. How many pulpits in this community defended racism as a component of the gospel? I went on to describe how individualism, consumerism, U.S. nationalism, and many other cultural characteristics have continually shaped the modern American understanding of the gospel.

In every era, culture and gospel are in constant collision. This will be true in the emerging culture, just as it has been true in every culture that preceded it. The gospel message will be shaped by the realities of the emerging culture. The question is: How will we respond?

Invitation to Conversation: Cultural Exegesis and an Expanded Gospel

The fear of cultural intrusion and the ideal of a culture-free gospel cannot drive the church's reflection as it enters the emerging culture. Instead, we need to learn skills of cultural exegesis that allow for the necessity of a culturally sensitive gospel while avoiding the distractions of inappropriate cultural infatuations.

By *cultural exegesis*, I mean a passionate and wary study of our surrounding culture. We should study our culture with enthusiasm and diligence because we believe the great mysteries of God and God's intentions are often revealed in our surrounding culture. (This is the historic Christian belief of "general revelation.") Our culture provides the framework and perspective we need in order to dialogue with, pray to, and wrestle with God. Yet we must also query our culture warily because it can certainly obscure the gospel. For example, the competition and consumerism that saturate American culture are regularly woven into our beliefs and practices. A cultural exegesis that explores these realities could not only warn us of their contaminating presence, but also could profoundly shape our proclamation of the gospel.

I experienced a more personal example of cultural exegesis several years ago. A few members of our congregation asked to meet with me to discuss their concerns about a sermon I'd preached, which included several sexual references and illustrations. They felt I'd included this material merely to heighten interest in a seemingly unrelated point in the sermon. One man commented that these illustrations had "made the gospel seem far less lofty and a bit dirty." I began my response by saying I didn't believe the gospel is lofty at all. Instead, it's quite "dirty" because it collides graciously with the fabric of our lives and culture. In that sermon I'd tried to point out how our entitled individualism often translates into moral autonomy and especially sexual autonomy in our lives ("God will just have to accept all of my moral and sexual choices!"). The sexual references in the sermon were intentional and missional, an effort to address how the "hook-up" sexual culture of our college town clashes with the communal expectations of the gospel. I felt an honest description of these realities could offer a fresh backdrop to sharpen our understanding of the graciousness of Jesus' ethical message. But these men offered me another cultural perspective that I needed to hear, reminding me to consider the sensitivities of younger kids who admire collegians uncritically. We left the evening with genuine embraces, greater wisdom, and a mutually heightened perspective about the meaning and power of the gospel in the breadth of community.

In an environment where cultural change has accelerated beyond all expectations, cultural exegesis is one of the most critical tools the church can use as it moves into the future. Careful study of the emerging culture can help shift our focus from fears of a culture-corrupted gospel to more productive questions of how our cultural sensitivities expand or obscure our understanding of a gospel that is simultaneously real, concrete, and practical, yet also infinite and mysterious.

There is little doubt that emerging culture presuppositions will at times obscure significant aspects of the gospel. I've heard the gospel described as shrouded so deeply in mystery that one would believe no aspect of the gospel was truly knowable. Such a passion for mystery can discourage specific responses to the gospel, such as worship, love and compassion for our neighbors, the hatred of injustice, and living a life of faith.

But these same cultural challenges also bring a potential passion—a demand, really—for the experience of an expanded gospel that comes far closer to the teachings and hopes of Jesus. Recently, Greg, a friend and seminarian, approached me with a simple request. He needed to "present the gospel" to me as a graded assignment for a class on evangelism. His presentation was immaculate—complete with key Scripture citations, a bridge diagram, and concise information to guide the listener to respond enthusiastically to Jesus' invitation to personal salvation. His professor had provided a list of required elements in the presentation, and Greg scored a perfect 100!

After he finished, Greg sat back and asked with a smile, "Now what do you really think about my presentation?" I first affirmed that he'd shared the "essence of the gospel" I'd been taught from childhood through seminary. I'd learned the very same presentation—literally the same verses, diagrams, and questions. But now I listen to this cherished presentation with a perspective shaped by an infinite number of cultural experiences—both inside and outside the church. Greg and I agreed that his presentation included a strong affirmation of personal salvation. But where were the affirmations about the community aspects of salvation (such as a freedom from shame and God's desire to redeem all of creation) and the calling to love our neighbors and combat social systems of injustice? There were many references to Christian doctrine, but little mention of spiritual formation or worship. The presentation included a consistent emphasis on the certainty of God's revelation, but no mention of the great mysteries of God that either inspire our worship or drive us to fear and doubt. This summary of the gospel was rooted in the eternal hope that Christ followers enjoy, but it offered no mention of the kingdom Jesus perpetually announced as taking shape in human history. Greg and I both acknowledged the truthfulness and accuracy of his presentation, but it certainly wasn't the whole gospel.

The emerging culture offers us the great challenge to pursue an expanded gospel. Shaped by our secular and individualistic culture, the gospel is reduced in a variety of ways. It becomes "a gospel of my lifestyle" (an affirmation of personal choices), "a gospel of my people" (an affirmation of national or local interests), "a gospel of my dreams" (an affirmation of our own aspirations and future plans), or "a gospel of my pain" (an affirmation of God's ability to heal our personal issues and pain). The emerging culture's interests in artistic beauty, holism, mystery, historical narrative and ritual, and community are expanding our understanding and application of the gospel. Each of these interests is reinforced and distinctively expressed in the teachings of Jesus and the narrative of the Scriptures.

This time of cultural transition—like every time of great social change—offers great opportunities for the church. In every cultural era, the message of the church faces the dual challenges of embellishment or reduction according to the interests of the culture. As we enter this new era of the emerging culture, we must seek ways in which the sensitivities of a new environment may expand our understanding of the gospel, while remaining alert to how portions of the gospel may be obscured by the interests of this culture.

CHAPTER THREE

Seven Deadly Fears and Seven Essential Conversations, Part 2: Scripture and Ethics

A deep commitment to the teachings of the Bible and a desire to live by a Christian ethic of behavior are central to our faith. Within the Christian community, beliefs about the Bible and ethics provoke great passion, accentuate internal divisions, and motivate much of the critique and dialogue regarding our surrounding culture. In other words, we'll fight over—even go to the wall for—our particular beliefs about the Scriptures and our moral expectations of one another. These are two citadels that we'll defend at all costs!

It comes as no surprise that the gathering tide of the emerging culture and the development of the emerging church have invigorated concerns about the Bible and ethics. Again, my desire is to move from simplistic, overstated fears that can paralyze us to conversations that can shape the church's transition into the emerging culture.

Transition doesn't require the church to dilute or divest itself from its most precious doctrines or values. But cultural transition can reveal that the Christian community places emphasis on peripheral concerns that undervalue the doctrine or values being defended. This is certainly the case with these two passions. If we can get past the simplistic fears that engagement with the emerging culture means "abandoning the Bible" and an "anything goes" approach to moral behavior, we'll see that the challenges of cultural transition provide the church great opportunity for growth in thought and practice.

WATERING DOWN THE WORD OF GOD

The fourth deadly fear: Ministry in the emerging culture leads to the devaluation of the Bible.

Commitment to Scripture is a hallmark of our faith. We at the Chapel Hill Bible Church have historically lived out our name through our passion for using the Scriptures as a catalyst for our ministries. In this environment, I've had more than a few conversations that begin something like this:

> Concerned Friend: (said with an embarrassed scowl)
> I hear you're leading an emerging culture initiative for
> the church.
>
> Me: Yes, I'm afraid that's true. (nervous chuckle)
>
> Concerned Friend: It just scares me that we are mini-
> mizing the importance of the Scriptures or watering
> down the teachings of the Bible.

Among certain portions of the church, there exists the disappointing assumption that engagement with the emerging culture
requires a devaluation of the Bible. (It should be noted that other
portions of the church fear emerging culture ministry as a Trojan
horse for a return to biblical literalism—which for these Christians
is a devaluation of the Bible.)

I have many reactions to these assumptions and fears. My first
reaction is to take them seriously. My own spiritual life has been
deeply confronted, formed, and encouraged by the Scriptures—so
naturally I hate to see the Bible devalued. During times when I'd
lost hope in the church, I found powerful solace in the Scriptures.
While in seminary, one assignment provoked a commitment to
read the gospels as narratives meditatively and repetitively. During this discipline, I experienced profound reorientation in several
aspects of my theology, gentle confrontation of many of my prejudices, a restoration of hope for God's work of redemption, and a
renewed love for the way of Jesus. My love for the Scriptures is
central to every aspect of my spiritual journey. And I believe the
Scriptures are critical for the spiritual health of the Christian community. Without a vital connection to God's story, and hence our
own story, we will wither.

But my second reaction is that when such fears are focused
entirely on the emerging culture, they tend to be misplaced. I've

been grieved to observe the Bible's devaluation in a variety of circumstances. In the fundamentalism of my childhood, the Bible was loved and accepted as an authority; but it was left largely unstudied and rarely interpreted. In my later exposure to the academy and to segments of the church that rely heavily on methods of higher criticism, I observed a Bible that was rigorously examined; yet its power was held in check by suspicions derived from the norms of scientific inquiry and expectations derived from secularism. At an evangelical seminary, I encountered a Bible that was studied diligently and utilized devotionally but it was also regularly held captive to the premises of systematic theology.[31] As a pastor and observer in a variety of church settings, I've lived with a Bible that has been highly valued but often trivialized by false expectations and assumptions about what it teaches.[32]

The Scriptures face marginalization—both in our culture and in the church. I strongly believe a dialogue energized by the assumptions of the emerging culture can provide a powerful response to this marginalization and devaluation. The possibilities of this dialogue are most visible when we consider some of the ways we limit the voice of the Bible.

Propositionalism

We devalue the Bible when we reduce it to a set of simple principles that can be easily communicated, understood, and acted upon. Some portions of the Bible are certainly very propositional. But whole genres of the Bible are ignored or damaged by an excess of this impulse: the rich and complex narratives of the Old Testament; the poetry, emotional intensity, metaphorical drama, and cultural commentary of the prophets; the artistry of the psalmists and wisdom writers; the mysticism of the apocalyptic writers; the documentary style and editorial genius of the gospel writers; and the historical and contextual sensitivity of the epistles.

---

[31] The message and interpretation of specific biblical texts were often organized by and limited to what was consistent with theological systems. We do this regularly in church life as well. I've been in several church environments that championed the importance of expository preaching that used extensive Bible study as its basis. In some of these settings, exposition amounted to drawing principles and propositions from various Bible passages to affirm a preferred belief or theological system.

[32] Common interpretations and expectations like, "I know I'll find a specific reason for my pain by studying the Bible" or "The Bible will show me exactly how to raise my kids or run my business" abound. So often these interpretations must be discredited and disavowed in pastoral counseling sessions before the wisdom and richness of the Scriptures can address the life context in question.

Propositionalism lends itself to teaching using memorable sound bites that belie the complexity of the Scriptures. The Bible becomes far too cognitive—a text that speaks only to our mind—and the holism of Scripture that touches our bodies, emotions, and relationships is limited or lost. The reduction of the biblical narrative and message into doctrinal or ethical propositions also provokes an air of certainty that trumps the mysteries of the Bible, as well as our need for continual study and contemplation of these sacred stories and words.

Moralism

Moralism is a form of propositionalism predominant enough to merit its own consideration. Moralism reduces the Bible to moral lessons and imperatives, robbing Scripture of its narrative quality. So much of the Bible is the scandalous story of humans asserting their own agendas or trying to accomplish God's agenda apart from God. Consider the story of Jacob, the decisions of the judges, or the struggles of the early church—all great narratives that reveal the magnitude, persistence, inevitability, and graciousness of God's redemptive work. But they include few moral lessons that can be simply incorporated into our decision-making.

The story of Esther offers a great example of the damage we can do to the Scriptures if we try to read them simply as a moral directive. During the Jewish nation's captivity under the Persians, a beautiful Jewish woman named Esther is placed in King Xerxes' harem and eventually becomes queen. Her status and favor with the king allows her not only to stave off a planned genocide of her people, but also to punish the people who plotted the destruction of Jews. This amazing story graphically portrays the sovereignty of God despite the greed and immorality of humanity.

But if we read it as a morality tale, we might draw the following lessons:

- Join a harem and things will go better for you and for those around you!

- If you are physically beautiful, you can rule the world. If not, better luck next time!
- Manipulation works—ask for favors the right way and you'll get your way!
- When you finally get the upper hand, use it as an iron fist and take revenge on those who have threatened you.

Moralism dehumanizes the characters of the Bible, blindly canonizes many of them into sainthood, and directs our attention away from the only hero of the Scriptures—God.[33]

The Bible as Cultural Chaplain

The Scriptures are devalued when they're used only to affirm and bless our culture and its characteristics. When the Bible becomes an "amen" to selfish politics, consumerism, individualism, the American way, and our many other cultural agendas, its radical message is silenced. The Bible becomes a weak-voiced pastor sitting at the cultural head table and offering a meaningless invocation—just happy to be in the room.

But the Jesus who shakes up the religious authorities by healing on the Sabbath, scandalizes the norms of his day by conversing with a Samaritan woman, frequents the table of tax collectors and other marginal persons, and says we meet the eternal God in the faces of the poor—this Jesus is silenced and excluded.

The God who sent Jonah to offer forgiveness to the most militant and unforgiving nation of the ancient world, who inspired the cultural wit and treason of the prophets, and who set up a theocracy that demanded cities of sanctuary and regular economic redistribution is left without a ticket to the banquet. And we're left with an invocation that blesses our appetites and excuses our failures, instead of the redemptive story that shakes human culture to its core and offers freedom from the lifestyles that are killing us.

---

[33] One great temptation to moralism comes in teaching children. See Ivy Beckwith in *Postmodern Children's Ministry* (Grand Rapids, Mich.: Zondervan, 2004) for an excellent treatment of this issue and its consequences in the spiritual formation of children.

Lost or Lazy Interpretation

Hermeneutics is the discipline and art of transporting the directives and narratives of the Scriptures from their original cultural contexts to our own contemporary contexts. Every time we encounter a command for women to cover their heads in worship, read directives about how to live as slaves or treat the slaves we own, or hear about avoiding idol feasts, we interpret the Scriptures (whether we admit it or not!). In a time when many fear "the loss of truth" or secularization, it doesn't appear as though the church is putting great effort into teaching or modeling thoughtful interpretation.

Our church constitution requires that we read aloud a text from 1 Timothy 3 on the Sunday we begin accepting annual nominations for the offices of elder and deacon. On a few occasions, we've just read this text about the qualifications of leaders and then gone on to describe how we select and utilize leaders. The text that states, "a deacon must be the husband of but one wife" (1 Timothy 3:12) sits like a beacon on the widescreen while we describe a process where women and single men are accepted as deacons. Our failure to follow the literal teaching of this text without offering any interpretation of its cultural nuances implies the interpretation is self-evident or doesn't matter—which defeats the purpose of reading it in the first place!

The costs of the loss of hermeneutics are high. A lack of effort in hermeneutics strips the Bible of its flexibility, its relevance, and its ability to speak into the fabric of our culture and lives with wisdom and power. The Bible becomes a sacred or an embarrassing anachronism, a beloved great-grandparent urging an action or possibility that no longer exists in the present.

Captivity to Systematic Theology

Sometimes our biblical interpretations are, in reality, a subjection of the Bible to the presuppositions and organizational needs of systematic theology. The great theological systems of the modern era (Reformed theology, dispensationalism, Wesleyanism, and other variants) reflect both the genius and the weaknesses of the Enlightenment. Systematic theology has offered us profound theological insights, but also reflects the Enlightenment characteristics and preoccupations of compartmentalization, reductionism, propositionalism, the objectivity of truth, and the scientific method. My office shelves are filled with the classic works of Calvin, Luther, Wesley, and their students, and I expect these teachings will continue to inform and bless the church in perpetuity. Yet the preeminence of systematic theology carries with it the danger that we may read the Bible for affirmation of our favored system, strip-mining the biblical narrative for verses, illustrations, and smaller segments that fit a prescribed theological package. The marvelous contours of the narrative forest are lost or ignored as we remove individual trees to be used as pillars of a theological system.

Systematics implies the complete coherence and understandability of the Bible as its points are placed neatly in a system of thought. This can rob Scripture not only of its narrative flow, but also its mystery, complexity, and internal dialogue. For example, the differing perspectives on Jesus' life offered by the four gospels create a diverse picture and provoke conversation about Jesus that broadens our view of him and adds great authenticity to the story. Combine Paul's concern about the impact of Jewish theology and practice on the church (found in Galatians and Romans) with Peter's embrace of the historical legacy and language of the Israelites in his first epistle, and together they form a rich and complex perspective of the church's relationship with Judaism. These complexities that draw us into thoughtful consideration and open dialogue about the Scriptures can too easily be erased by hard-and-fast systems.

The Bible as a Symbol or Object of Worship

The Bible is sometimes used as a symbol of reverence, orthodoxy, theological purity, national pride, or spiritual maturity. Years ago we saw evidence of this when our elders at the Chapel Hill Bible Church initiated a process to change our name. We were concerned it was a barrier to ministry in our community and that it implied the

Bible was the object of our worship. In a lively open forum about this topic, one well-intended person bemoaned, "We can't change our name. We've got to have something from the Bible in our name. And, of course, 'Bible' is in the Bible!" An impolite, though accurate, response would have been to point out that the word Bible is only on the cover and never actually appears in the text itself! But the intense passion behind his sentiment stemmed from the fact that the Bible was being employed as a symbol for our history (our historical name), our style of ministry (a Bible-teaching church), and our theological orthodoxy (to differentiate us from churches whom we perceive to value the Bible less than we do).

For many Christians, the Bible serves as a symbol of God's grace and personal nature (a God who reveals and speaks). For others in our culture, however, it's a symbol of ignorance, prejudice, and false hope. In a culture transitioning from some measure of a Christian consensus to a post-Christian consciousness, the Bible will remain a symbolic battleground. When our use of the Bible is highly symbolic or our defense of the Bible implies that it's an object of worship, our energy and attention is drawn away from the story and heart of the Scriptures. Tragically, I believe the vehement and sometimes misguided Christian defense of the Bible causes it to be seen as a symbolic caricature for a belief system or political perspective, rather than what it truly is—the great narrative of the historical faithfulness and activity of a loving and redeeming God.

Invitation to Conversation: The Bible as Inclusive and Confronting Narrative

Emerging culture passions of community, beauty, mystery, holism, and story (particularly local narratives) offer significant possibilities for a Bible that has faced increasing marginalization. This is not to say the Bible won't face new challenges in the emerging culture. It certainly will. The perspectives of every cultural environment threaten to become prejudices that limit our vision and expectations. For example, it's easy to imagine settings where the predisposition to see mystery in Scriptures will obscure clear instruction in the Bible that is to be obeyed specifically. There is a possibility that sensitivity to the specific historical context of particular biblical narratives could minimize a culturally transcendent message.

But as those who read, adore, and listen to biblical texts enter into the emerging culture, there is great potential for new and liberating approaches to Scripture to arise. As the modern era collides with the emerging culture, the Bible can be rediscovered as an inclusive narrative that speaks with power and relevance to both cultural understandings. The tension of multiple cultural perspectives might serve as a deterrent against the potential limitations and prejudices of a single cultural viewpoint, making us more open to the strengths that can be found in each approach.

In our time of cultural collision and transition, we can rediscover a Bible that presents timeless truths as well as deep mysteries that require the patient posture of faithfulness. Our exegesis can emphasize the local stories of faith in specific contexts, while remaining open to meaning that transcends culture. Clear propositions in the Bible can be affirmed while space is allowed to celebrate equally its stories, poems, songs, and mystical visions. An analysis of the whole biblical message should help us develop new patterns of thought that speak to the emerging culture (and affirm and challenge some aspects of our existing systematic theologies). Interest in the local contexts and specific implications of the varied parts of the Bible should also allow us to create tension and humility in our theological systems, ensuring that these systems serve the Bible rather than dominate our reading and interpretation.

Understanding the Bible as a narrative that is inclusive of the perspectives of many cultural perspectives (emerging, modern, and pre-modern) will demand both the meticulous analysis and exegesis of the modern era and interpretative methods that are contemplative, meditative, and historical. As an inclusive narrative, the primary contexts of interpretation will not just be a pastor in a study, a scholar in a library, or a person of faith alone in devotion. The diverse communities of our own culture will join their voices with the historical communities that gave birth to these texts and have read them with love and interest through the ages.

The Bible as an inclusive narrative will be larger and speak with a more powerful voice to our cultures and communities. The Bible's narrative can also confront us with the dangers of our age and a call to live in new ways. Rather than blessing our culture and affirming the appetites it encourages, the Bible can speak with passion, warning, and prophetic vision to us. Scripture can guide us to a vision of community, wholeness, redemption, and eternity that confronts and surpasses the dreams of our culture. The prophetic voice of the Scriptures will be directed not only to individuals but also to our social and ethnic communities and political and economic systems. Its message of redemption and liberation will be heard as it was intended—a powerful vision of hope for individuals, communities, nations, and all of creation.

In this transition, we have opportunity to rediscover the Bible as a sacred text with a diversity, voice, and scope that are far greater than the many limits we place upon it.

CONDONING PERSONAL IMMORALITY AND THE ABANDONMENT OF CHRISTIAN ETHICS

The fifth deadly fear: Ministry in the emerging culture means abandoning Christian ethics and accepting immoral behavior.

When our church was preparing to launch its emerging culture initiative, we decided to spend a Sunday service discussing our plans. Somewhere in the congregation, a prominent lay leader whispered the following questions to a neighbor: "What will they do about sexual immorality? Will they be silent? Will they even care? Will the high ethical standards of Christianity be thrown away for the sake of mission and relevance?" These questions reveal a common fear and widely held assumption about the church's intention to minister in the emerging culture.

A few months before this same presentation, I'd preached a series of sermons entitled, "Are We Really the Good Guys?" That title mirrors a question continually directed at the church by an increasingly post-Christian culture. I had little difficulty finding evidence of our culture's moral concern about Christianity. Dan Brown's huge bestseller, *The Da Vinci Code*, raised questions about sexual repression in the church, as well as the church's effort to control the writing of history in order to substantiate its power and theological claims. Through this novel, the words of Leonardo Da Vinci were once again being volleyed at the Christian establishment:

> Many have made a trade of delusion and false miracles, deceiving the stupid multitude...Blinding ignorance does mislead us. O! Wretched mortals, open your eyes.[34]

Around this same time, the *New York Times* and other sources were reporting a battle between Alabama Governor Bob Riley and Christian political conservatives over the state's highly regressive income tax. Riley was seeking to change the state's tax code, which allowed for the nation's highest rate of taxation among the poor (even on groceries and baby items!) while also offering significant tax relief for corporations and those with the highest incomes.[35] While Governor Riley said his reading of the New Testament was part of his inspiration for changing the tax code, the Christian conservatives were entrenched firmly on the other side of this issue.[36]

Living in a politically liberal university community, I often hear criticisms that the Christian church is silent, unconcerned, or just plain wrong about issues of poverty, social systems of injustice, violence and war, the environment, and human sexuality. Perhaps singer/songwriter Tori Amos, a preacher's daughter, offered one of the most succinct and acidic summaries of these accusations in an interview where she implored Christians "to lighten up on the savior bit, folks. You know, get off the cross, we need the wood!"[37]

---

[34] Cited by Dan Brown, *The Da Vinci Code* (New York: Doubleday, 2003), 231.

[35] *NYTimes.com* article by Adam Cohen, "What Would Jesus Do? Sock It to Alabama's Corporate Landowners" (June 10, 2003).

[36] Christian social activist Jim Wallis cited this same battle during the 2003 Emergent Convention in San Diego. The Christian Right's position on this debate prompted him to quip that perhaps the New Testament had not quite made its way to Alabama!

[37] *Spin* magazine article by Charles Aaron, "Sex, God, and Rock 'n' Roll" (October 1994).

These illustrations highlight the battle line that's been drawn between the existing church and the emerging culture. Each side of this battlefront accuses the other of immorality. While many in the church decry the rising immorality of our culture, the culture returns the same accusation at the church. The frequently angry tone of this dialogue has become one of the most critical determinants of the church's ability to enter the emerging culture with credibility.

Many in the Christian establishment contend that media and cultural prejudices stoke these accusations about the church. I vividly remember the disappointment in the voice of a local reporter when I refused to supply him with a litany of angry and sanctimonious quotes about a "sacrilegious" photography exhibit that made a tour stop in Chapel Hill years ago. He was seeking a strident Christian voice of damnation to help make his article more entertaining and controversial. Too often the Christian establishment—conservative and liberal—has accepted caricatured and stereotypical roles in public and media discourse about ethical and social issues.

The criticism that the Christian community cares little about social concerns is decidedly inaccurate. Catholics, Anglicans, and mainline Protestants have a long history of activism around issues of social justice. These believers rightly bridle and chafe when lumped together with conservative Christians in critiques of the church's insensitivity, silence, or moral error on social issues. In the past, the conservative wing of the church left itself open to the critique that it was interested in "saving souls" at the expense of alleviating human suffering and meeting social needs. But evangelicals can point now to the copious relief and social organizations they've founded, supported, and populated in recent decades. The foyers and worship bulletins of many evangelical churches include numerous opportunities to serve in social causes. Social justice has been an area of historic strength for one portion of the existing church and of significant expansion for another.[38]

Nonetheless, I believe the Christian community needs to acknowl-

---

[38] I will comment directly on this liberal-conservative divide in Christianity and its impact on the church's entry into the emerging church in the next chapter. But if you are interested in the roots of this division and the particular causes of separation over social issues, I would recommend George Marsden's *Fundamentalism and American Culture* (New York: Oxford University Press, 1980). His attention to the theological and social antecedents of this divide is excellent and very readable.

edge that there is some truth to the emerging culture's criticism of us. When we honestly listen to the ethical critiques that the emerging culture has levied at the church (even when these critiques are heavy-handed or not entirely accurate), certain weaknesses and blind spots in our ethical message appear. Two topics strongly illustrate this point: homosexuality and race.

Homosexuality: The Danger of a Single-Issue Ethic

Currently, homosexuality is the lightning rod of conflict, both within the church and in the church's conversation with the larger society about moral issues. When charges of "immorality" are made, the issue of homosexuality often lurks just below the surface. Stances on gay marriage, the ordination of homosexual clergy, and the simple freedom of homosexuals to participate in the Christian community have become the new litmus tests for orthodoxy, belief in the authority of Scripture, and the ability to resist cultural indoctrination.

Some Christians believe the acceptance and affirmation of gay or lesbian persons in some church congregations is the ultimate example of capitulation to an immoral society.[39] Conversely, many outside the church believe that the church's perceived intolerance and lack of compassion toward homosexuals is the ultimate indictment on the church's character.

The inordinate amount of attention placed on the topic of homosexuality (and the tone of our dialogue!) dulls the church's very significant message on the larger topic of human sexuality. Sexuality is reflective of both God's marvelous creative intent and the most essential spiritual realities of mutuality, community, and intimacy—yet such theological exploration is lost in our emphasis on homosexuality.[40]

Other important ethical issues related to gender and sexuality—such as pornography, the increasing feminization of poverty, the early sexualization of children in our culture, inappropriate sexual stereotypes, promiscuity, prejudices related to physical beauty,

---

[39] The Christian community is certainly not unified on this issue and its implications.

[40] Scripture has much to say about human sexuality. The first description of humanity in Genesis 1:27 is that we are sexual beings (having gender, male and female) and spiritual beings (made in God's image, hence we are able to know and relate to God). Our sexuality and spirituality are intertwined like the double helix of human DNA. This reality has tremendous implications for community formation, yet these issues are often lost when our debate of homosexuality dominates the bandwidth of our dialogue on sexuality.

and the implicit racism in our notions of beauty—suffer from minimal attention. Most grievously, we are often silent on ethical issues related to heterosexual behavior. The strong disconnect and disassociation of homosexuality from heterosexuality allows some Christians to decry homosexual behavior as immoral, while ignoring many of the same issues of promiscuity and pain in relation to heterosexuality.[41]

The church will continue to struggle with this topic. Yet the nature of our dialogue on homosexuality illustrates the danger of reducing our ethical conversations to a specific issue. Our passion toward singular issues like homosexuality forces us to continually answer cultural indictments of intolerance (largely due to a media and cultural focus on the worst of our dialogue on the subject) and irrelevance (as we seemingly ignore other important ethical concerns).

Racism: The Danger of Individualism

A brief examination of racism reveals a second blind spot. The church has long been criticized for its racial segregation. It's often been said that 11 a.m. is the most segregated hour of the week. Although some congregations and Christian organizations are undertaking the challenging and biblical path of multiethnicity, many U.S. churches continue to reflect the racial divisions in their communities and the broader culture.

Recent research on race and Christianity offers some valuable insights about the connection between racism and individualism. In their excellent book, *Divided by Faith: Evangelical Religion and the Problem of Race in America*, sociologists Michael Emerson and Christian Smith conclude that evangelical theology's emphases on personal salvation and individual free will accentuate the racial divide in the church. The evangelical focus on personal faith and privatized religion encourages inadequate, individualistic solutions to a systemic social problem like racism. The predisposition to solve the world's ills one person or soul at a time invites inattentiveness and insensitivity to racism and other structural injustices. A highly

---

[41] For example, how many pulpits have spent comparable energy in addressing marital unfaithfulness? While traveling in East Africa, I saw an "altar call" where the pastor asked any who had been unfaithful to their spouses in any manner during the last year to stand up and seek forgiveness. To my shock and surprise, many stood up. I'm not sure I would try that approach. But I appreciate the courage and concern of this pastor!

individualized theology can also prevent cooperation between majority culture congregations and minority congregations (which tend to place more attention on systemic evils and injustice).[42]

Emerson and Smith's observations on race and theology can be applied to other ethical concerns. Although the tendency is more pronounced in evangelicalism, a spirit of individualism has seeped into the theology, ethical teaching, and programs of many U.S. congregations across the theological spectrum. The high emphasis on community within the emerging culture results in a quick and incisive criticism of the individualism that infuses our theology and our ethics. This is a criticism the church needs to hear.

Invitation to Conversation: Personal and Corporate Ethics

The ethical challenges and critiques that the postmodern emerging culture directs at Christianity offer an opportunity for productive dialogue. Our emerging culture's interest in corporate and social ethics and the church's tendency to focus on personal ethics typically yields debate that is characterized by misunderstanding and bitter incriminations. A restored interest in corporate ethics in the church and openness to dialogue with the emerging culture on questions of personal and social ethics can have tremendous results for the church's mission.

Reclaiming an interest in corporate ethics not only invites a more productive conversation with the emerging culture, it also offers the church the opportunity to rediscover lost emphases from our own authoritative text and history. The Scriptures are filled with systemic ethical concerns and directives that are startling to read in the context of our highly individualized culture. The Old Testament is filled with teaching and practices that model a deep concern for social justice: provisions are made for the care and protection of widows and orphans; sanctuary and refuge is offered to those in legal disputes; the poor are fed by the gleaning of others' fields; and Jubilee practices protected the earth from overuse and abuse and placed a buffer on the accumulation of wealth.

[42] Michael O. Emerson and Christian Smith, *Divided by Faith: Evangelical Religion and the Problem of Race in America* (New York: Oxford University Press, 2000).

The Scriptures also remind us that personal ethics are deeply enhanced by social and communal sensitivities. Paul's discourse on sexual ethics in 1 Corinthians 6:12-20 connects personal sexual choices to the broader theology of our mystical, relational connection with Christ (and thus the community joined to Christ). The imperative against sexual promiscuity not only makes more sense, but also has a heightened significance when placed in this corporate and communal context.

The history of the church is filled with times of great concern about and intervention against social evils and injustices. Our Scriptures provide historical narrative, common-sense wisdom, and liberating theology that speak to both personal and corporate ethics. If the church hopes to transition into the emerging culture with credibility, relevance, and authenticity, then a broadened interest and vision for social ethics is an absolute necessity.

Surely, the church is right to cherish and defend the Bible and Christian ethics. Yet our reduction of the Scriptures to a book of moral lessons and our limitation of the social significance of our ethical message tends to undermine, rather than defend, these precious distinctives we cherish. The questions and criticisms of the emerging culture invite the church to rediscover the breadth of the Scripture narratives and utilize our sacred text with greater relevance, influence, and voice in our culture. An expanded social ethic goes hand in hand with this recovery of the Bible's social message, bringing us back in line with lost portions of our history and a core commitment of our own theology.

These theological conversations are vital if the church would transition into effective engagement with the emerging culture. The fearful oversimplification that emerging culture ministry equals the devaluation of the Bible and personal ethics being jettisoned derails these opportunities for growth.

CHAPTER FOUR

Seven Deadly Fears and Seven Essential Conversations, Part 3: Christian Traditions

The church landscape in our culture has changed radically over the last couple of decades. Many traditional churches have started "contemporary" worship services. Other churches that have been more informal in style are now exploring a more fixed liturgy and new worship symbols. New designs for staffing and church organization abound. We are transforming the language of worship, spiritual growth, and relationships. The examples of change in church life seem almost limitless.

Some of these changes have been visionary or mission-driven. Others have been motivated by cultural trends, demographic transition, competition, market targeting, and the growing sense among some churches that they are being left behind. These transitions and new experiments have left many churchgoers feeling very unsettled. They wonder if all that is familiar is up for negotiation. They worry that the theological essentials their churches were founded upon are now eroding under their feet.

As I've insisted in the two previous chapters, I believe the changes of the emerging culture both demand transition for the church and offer splendid opportunities for introspection and growth in our understanding and embodiment of the gospel. Nevertheless, I understand that this torrent of change can be dizzying. During one five-year period at Chapel Hill Bible Church, we experienced the retirement of the founding/teaching pastor, significant changes in our worship and teaching style, a move to a much larger facility, a near doubling of our average attendance, and the hiring of many new staff members. What's more, we were asked to join an intentional conversation about emerging culture mission and transition. It's a lot, to say the least. And we aren't alone in experiencing this volume of change. In fact, I believe our experience is quite common.

The pace and substance of change in contemporary church life lead to two areas of fear regarding the loss of Christian traditions from the existing church as it sits at the threshold of the emerging culture. The first involves the loss of familiar practices; the second, the loss of a theological heritage.

THE CHURCH ENVIRONMENT AND THE LOSS OF TRADITION

The sixth deadly fear: Transition to ministry in the emerging culture means the loss of the traditions and practices we hold dear.

This fear includes losses related to changes in music and hymnody, adaptations of other elements of worship services, the loss of sacred language describing fellowship and spirituality, the marginalization or departure of beloved leaders who feel uncomfortable in a changed church environment, transitions in church polity and structure, new facilities, or simply a change in the weekly church calendar. Any one of these changes can feel tremendously unsettling for participants in a local fellowship—the possibility of numerous simultaneous changes can make church members fear their religious traditions are being torn right out from under their feet. Both the emerging culture and emerging church have been catalysts and convenient scapegoats for this concern. The truth is a bit more complicated.

In Chapel Hill the discussion about hiring a new worship pastor and the possible changes in our worship style that could result prompted one church member to voice his concerns in an open congregational discussion. This church member, who happened to be white, exclaimed that he felt like we were rethinking all of our traditions. This generalization prompted an African-American staff member to retort, "Whose traditions are you talking about? I don't ever remember our using *my* own traditions."

This interchange illustrates the basic problem when talking about tradition. The word traditional is meaningless without a frame of reference. What is tradition to one person is an innovation, a whim, a distant memory, or an oddity to another. In our transitory, melting-pot society, even most racially and culturally homogenous churches are far too diverse to use the term *tradition* in any more than a local sense. Typically, when we decry the loss of tradition, we mean we're losing the way things used to be done around here—at least in the recent past. The word tradition is used regularly to denote the recent past and decisions that stand outside essential historical or theological roots.[43]

This clarification is not intended to minimize the frustration or real angst involved when our traditions are ended or adapted. As I've shared, our church has experienced numerous changes—both intentional and unintentional—over a very short period of time. These changes were significant and very painful for many. There can be a tendency among those who like the new forms to discredit the pain of transitions. But the pain is real.

In his excellent book on community, *The Search to Belong*, Joe Myers explains that humans connect intimately to each other in four different spaces. One is what he calls the "public" sphere. In this sphere we make connections with others through common allegiances (like politics, products, or sports teams), gathering with a crowd in familiar places that are appreciated, and regular encounters with familiar faces in our daily routines.[44] I've realized that for many in our fellowship, our church's many changes have produced severe disruption in this public sphere intimacy. These pains should not be ridiculed or underestimated.

But there is another equally important set of losses that we experience as our worship communities change. These losses involve unspoken traditions or values that are often far more significant to us than more obvious outward changes—and are often the true motivation behind our anger or fear when a church's music or schedule changes. These traditions remain unspoken for a variety of reasons. Sometimes we're unaware of the significance these traditions hold in our expectations and hopes. Other times we're simply embarrassed by their value to us. Perhaps some of our unspoken values are even inconsistent with the values of the historical and scriptural Christian community. (In fact, many of these unspoken traditions could stand to be threatened.)

There's a Christian media outlet that uses the tagline, "Safe for the whole family." I understand what they're trying to say. But ev-

---

[43] This tends to be true even in Christian traditions and denominations that are liturgical, confessional, or draw upon a long historical tradition. Most likely, these historical and foundational roots are not up for negotiation. The changes that would cause fear and frustration would be similar to those that I mentioned previously.

[44] Joseph Myers, *The Search to Belong* (Grand Rapids, Mich.: Zondervan, 2003), 39-44.

ery time I hear that line, I want to mutter a rebuttal that the gospel really *isn't* safe for the whole family. Often, if we are honest with ourselves, our primary resistance to change in the church stems from the fact that we don't feel comfortable with that transition. Comfort and safety are two of our most common, unspoken values. In certain circumstances each can be appropriate, but neither one is a biblically ordained "given" in our lives of faith and community. Consider God's call of Abraham to journey to a distant land (Genesis 12:1-3). God offers great promises of the formation of a nation that will be used to redeem the world. But there is no assurance of comfort or safety in this challenging call.

Another unspoken value is certainty. Certainty can operate like an ethereal holy grail or a sacred untouchable in our churches. We constantly search for certainty. We lethally attack those who question it. I had a close friend who was almost fired for expressing a controversial theological position in a sermon. His position, though uncommon for his church's pulpit, was certainly not implausible and was familiar to many in this congregation. When the crisis finally blew over, a church board member confessed that the real issue wasn't the theological point the pastor had made. The real concern was that this challenge to the majority position on this particular issue would undermine the church's aura of certainty over other issues. Apparently, right or wrong, certainty must be maintained and protected in that fellowship.

Unspoken traditions are not confined to churches with long histories and memories. In some emerging churches I've visited, being culturally "cool" takes a prominent seat at the banquet of values. I once asked several attendees in an emerging church setting about an interesting and meaningful piece of art displayed in their meeting place. The theological possibilities for this piece seemed endless. But their response was that they had no clue what the piece meant or why it was in their worship space—but it sure was *cool*!

The list of values and traditions that sail beneath the surface, yet drive numerous decisions in our churches, is nearly unlimited.

I've only mentioned a few. The biblical narratives challenge or refine many of these values like safety, comfort, familiarity, certainty, and "coolness." Abraham's journey was from safety, comfort, and familiarity toward uncertainty. Noah's obedience in building an ark fell outside not only the boundaries of certainty, but also the bounds of all common sense and reason. Jacob strikes me as a leading character who was a bit cool—but on his great escape from home and his long return to Bethel, he seemed constantly out of sorts with God's will and even God's inevitable blessing. The prophets were poetic, dramatic, and honest. Their messages and lifestyles constantly contradicted the dominant values of safety, comfort, certainty—and even cool.

The pain involved in the change or loss of valued traditions can be very real. We should also realize that some of the traditions we defend—consciously or unconsciously—are inconsistent with the biblical narrative and the essence of our faith. Instead of clinging desperately to the traditions of our past, may we find ways to stay true to the best of our history and traditions, while forever remaining open to the new horizons to which God is calling us.

Invitation to Conversation: Finding Our History While Moving into Our Future

Ministry in the emerging culture is not simply about abandoning our traditions. It's about finding our history and connecting this legacy to our current and future mission. It's a great opportunity to deepen the spirituality of the church beyond simply our "near-past traditions" and to challenge many of the unspoken values that lay beneath these traditions.

When I was growing up in an independent church outside of Charlotte, North Carolina, I was deeply attentive to our church's practices and teachings. Our church had an altar call at every formal gathering so congregants could receive salvation or recommit their lives to following Christ. The walk down the aisle always ended with a firm and warm handshake with our pastor. I walked that aisle many times (I needed it), and that handshake remains a vivid memory of my childhood. But when I attended other churches, I noticed many of them (even the ones that seemed acceptable to my parents!) didn't have an altar call. I appreciated the warmth and directness of our practice, but I also began to question its theological significance and the emphasis we placed on this aspect of our worship. I remember asking my parents, "How can one handshake change the eternal fate of a person?" If the Harry Potter series had been around then, I might have asked how this handshake became some form of "portkey" to heaven. Something seemed odd to me about a worship tradition that was so important (we're talking about eternity here!), yet it wasn't universally practiced. Surely there should be some form of minor explosion—or at least a few sparks—when folks walked that aisle and shook the pastor's hand!

Many years later, thanks to the patience of several extremely gifted spiritual directors, my own spiritual practices have come to include liturgical prayer and praying the hours or daily offices. These experiences have been incredibly significant and liberating in my spiritual journey. I love to contemplate and breathe a prayer that has been crafted outside my own words and experiences and embraced by the church for hundreds or even thousands of years. I am encouraged by the realization that Christians all over the world are gathering at a similar hour to enjoy the same or similar prayers.

When I think of this joy, I begin to understand my current discomfort with the "handshake salvation" of my childhood. It wasn't the altar call—altar calls have their own significant and fruitful legacy in a segment of church history. It was the disconnectedness and isolation of this experience from other Christian traditions and from an ongoing life of faith. Our independent fellowship sometimes operated as if it were "independent" from the rest of the Christian community. Our practices felt entirely developed and contrived by our own community. Following the path of Jesus was extremely hard for me. There were many costs and many blunders. Though I did not have the words to express it, I wanted and needed a larger community to help me on the way. Given the recent rush of Christians to more liturgical practices, I know I'm not alone in this craving.

The emerging culture brings to us passions for finding our roots in historical narrative, community and social connectedness, and symbols. Building on these passions, the emerging church is developing community practices and worship experiences that explore the historical narrative of our faith, rediscovering spiritual disciplines that have been lost in some portions of the church, and creating new symbols that connect us with the richness of our past.

We are recovering elements of the Christian journey that have often been lost or minimized. In many, many Christian traditions, it's almost as if we think Christian history begins with the New Testament, jumps straight to the Reformation, and then skips another four centuries to the present era. When this is the case, we lose the rich traditions and lessons of the Desert Fathers. We lose the monasticism, mysticism, and scholasticism of the Middle Ages. Untold numbers of scholars, pastors, and spiritual contemplatives disappear from our story.

Not only that, but also we often operate as if the church were not an extension of the legacy and promise of the Judaism into which Jesus was born and out of which the church was founded. In 1 Peter 2:9-10, the marvelous Jewish descriptions of spiritual community are applied to the fledgling bands of persecuted and disorganized Christians throughout Asia Minor. Peter tells these Christ followers:

> But you are a chosen people, a royal priesthood, a holy nation, a people belonging to God, that you may declare the praises of him who called you out of darkness into his wonderful light. Once you were not a people, but now you are the people of God; once you had not received mercy, but now you have received mercy.

These are words right out of the vocabulary of the Old Testament—the great declarations of the identity of the Jewish people as being God's people. It's hard to imagine bolder words of affirmation and encouragement. Peter tells these early Christians they are part of a grand story, inheritors of an amazing legacy. This legacy implies not only their present reality (which seemed a bit tenuous) but also a great future destination (which surely felt unthinkable). These gracious words of identity are followed by Peter's immense summary of the mission of the church in 1 Peter 2:11-12:

> Dear friends, I urge you, as aliens and strangers in the world, to abstain from sinful desires, which war against your soul. Live such good lives among the pagans that, though they accuse you of doing wrong, they may see your good deeds and glorify God on the day he visits us.

Our historic identity is inextricably connected to and gives shape to our mission. The mission and promise of Christian community is easily misshapen without a deep understanding of history and the grand narrative of God's redemptive work of forming a people.

The church's transition into the emerging culture can be a journey of rediscovery of our history and reconnection with the wider Christian community. Our mission can be refined, expanded, and empowered by its reconnection to our historical identity. Many of the traditions we faithfully maintain can be enlivened with new understanding by their own reconnections with our historical story.

Our conversation with history should be both a gracious and a discerning dialogue. As we look to the past, we will find some historically bound events that will need to be accepted in their context and graciously interpreted as they speak into contemporary situations and questions. The realization that the church's story is filled with many mistakes and failures will encourage us to be discerning as we explore the past.

As we step into this emerging culture, I hope for a church that embraces its whole history and realizes that it—the church—isn't the whole story. Through a closer examination of our legacy, both distant and recent, may we be moved to tears of confession, expressions of repentance, greater understanding of God's redemptive work, bolder steps of mission, and greater hope.

CHURCH HERITAGE AND THE LOSS OF IDENTITY

The seventh deadly fear: Transition to ministry in the emerging culture demands that a church abandon its distinctive theological identity as liberal or conservative.

Before leaving the topic of tradition, I want to raise a critical question about the loss of theological heritage that has at times threatened to overwhelm the church's dialogue with the emerging culture. By theological heritage, I mean specifically the strong identity that many Christians and congregations have as either liberals or evangelicals.

I fondly remember a very honest statement I heard at a theological consortium at a historically liberal seminary more than a decade ago. We were participating in a study examining the impact of post-baby-boom generations on the church. One contributor was emphasizing the growing significance of historical Christian symbolism, Scripture, and the person of Jesus in future ministry. A pastor in a mainline denomination, poking fun at the reluctance of some congregations to focus on the ministry and teachings of Jesus, laughingly added, "We are going to have to get comfortable with the J-word again!" Another pastor responded instinctively and passionately, "As long as we can still be liberals!" to the great amusement of the group and speaker.

I have spent most of my professional ministry in evangelical settings, so I typically hear the other side of the same story. I've heard some evangelicals justify their support for an outside project simply by saying, "They're evangelicals." Assessing the quality of the idea or vision sometimes seems less important than finding a respected evangelical who endorses the concept. I've sometimes been amused to hear visitors from an outside ministry come to our congregation and trip all over themselves trying to prove they are real members of the "evangelical team."

For more than a century, segments of the church have been locked in a theological cold war that has defined the very essence of our congregations, practices, and convictions. This cold war has dominated our identity—determining what political candidates to support, what seminaries are trustworthy, what organizations to support and avoid, and what leaders are credible. Sociologist Robert Wuthnow, writing in *The Restructuring of American Religion*, explains the importance of the religious divide between liberals and conservatives:

> For American religion, this cleavage has become increasingly apparent as a new basis of differentiation not only between, but also within, major religious bodies...At present, the two sides seem to be deeply divided, comprising almost separate religious communities whose differences have become far more important than those associated with denominational traditions.[45]

Part of Wuthnow's thesis is that American religion has restructured itself around its liberal or conservative identities. For many Protestants, there are only two denominations that matter—liberal and conservative. This "two-party system" for American religion has resulted in significant territorialism, distrust, defensiveness, and competition.

I grew up on a country highway where almost everyone had a gravel driveway with a gentle downhill slope connecting home to the road. After a storm, the run-off from the rain would create deep trenches and ruts in our driveway. Riding our bikes was suddenly transformed from simple transportation to an extreme sport.

---

[45] Robert Wuthnow, *The Restructuring of American Religion* (Princeton, NJ.: Princeton University Press, 1988), 316.

(I still have a few scars to prove it!) We all welcomed the sight of my grandfather's small tractor when he'd come to generously scrape and manicure our driveway after the storms.

During the last several decades, the church landscape has become like our old driveway after a huge storm—rutted and treacherous. An atmosphere of fears and accusations is one of the legacies of the conservative-liberal cold war. Many conservative evangelicals use church expansion in attendance, finances, and facilities as the ultimate measure in order to claim a great victory in this war. Some liberals, looking at many highly profiled moral and financial fiascos among evangelicals, warn of the costs of "success" and claim their own victory, albeit by different measures. The harshest legacy is that new thoughts, prophetic visions, and expressions of Christianity are forced to fit into one of these two ruts. It's a lot like moving into our community of Chapel Hill and Durham. We'll be nice to you for about six months, but ultimately we're going to demand that you choose a basketball team—Duke or Carolina! You must choose—and you can't choose both!

The liberal-conservative polarity can produce a great deal of institutional insensitivity to the passions of the emerging culture and harsh verdicts about the emerging church. I was talking to a group of friends who are recent, gifted seminary graduates, and they are struggling with their job searches. They no longer fit into the neatly divided categories of either liberal or evangelical. Thus, they feel as though they are being pushed toward dishonesty throughout the interview processes.

Emerging culture passions are often quickly forced into evangelical-liberal categories and the related fears. I have a few friends who are respected members of our community, but with whom I can't seem to discuss our dreams for emerging culture ministry. When I begin talking about emerging church possibilities—such as community, appreciation of the contexts of the Scripture narratives, and corporate ethics as witness—they hear a rejection of personal salvation, a movement away from biblical authority, and a politicizing of the gospel. These are all evangelical fears and critiques of classical liberalism. Some of these friends are still fighting the fight.

I was perplexed and a bit wounded after leading a communion service in our church a few years ago. We often appropriately connect the celebration of communion with the resurrection of Jesus. But my morning's sermon had been on Jesus' birth and the significance of the incarnation—God taking on human flesh. In the communion meditation, I emphasized a celebration of the infinite love and grace involved in Jesus' willingness to submit to the incarnation. The next day, I received a sharply critical note charging that I'd abandoned our theological essentials in our practice of communion.

At first, I was mystified by this critique. My words on the incarnation were very consistent with the historical beliefs of our fellowship. But later, as I placed this criticism into the categories of the liberal-conservative divide, I began to understand the trajectory of the accusation. This person was used to an older, liberal theology that rejected the supernatural elements of the Bible, including the historicity of the resurrection. In his background in mainline churches, the theological lessons in the birth of Jesus were often exalted over the miracle of the resurrection. My words on incarnation in a resurrection context inflamed his fears of a return to the liberalism he had rejected. He, too, was still fighting the fight.

The liberal-conservative cold war has threatened to overwhelm the church's dialogue with the emerging culture and to polarize the innovations of the emerging church. But the emerging culture brings great news. There are many signs that although the battles have not ceased, the war is ending.

Invitation to Conversations: A Reshaped Orthodoxy

Like the rabid basketball fans in our North Carolina community, continually we've asked those who would follow Christ to choose either the liberal or the evangelical team. It reminds me of the episode in *The Lord of the Rings* where the hobbits, Merry and Pippin, ask the ancient forest guardian, Treebeard, whose side he is on in the brewing war of the ring. Treebeard wisely retorts that he is on no one's side because he is not sure if anyone is on the side of the forests![46] Many leaders and participants in the emerging church, including my friends who are searching for their first jobs out of seminary, feel like Treebeard. We're looking for another alternative. And the emerging culture offers the possibility of new missional options.

The old fault line between liberals and evangelicals is eroding. The questions and issues that produced the cold war are waning in relevance as we enter this new historical context. We're simply less prone to fight over a literal six-day creation, evolution, biblical inerrancy, and many of the other flashpoints of the last century. This doesn't mean the church, coming from conservative or liberal trajectories into the emerging culture, will no longer care about these issues. But a changed culture is transforming our perspectives on many of these questions.

Fuller Seminary philosopher, Nancey Murphy, writing in *Beyond Liberalism and Fundamentalism*, explains in great detail how the liberalism and fundamentalism of the last century were differing theological responses to a modern philosophical perspective— foundationalism. The conservative and liberal positions were both foundational, although they were constructed on radically differing foundations. (Conservatives used an inerrant and scientifically validated Bible as their foundation; liberals utilized religious experience as their foundation.) The emerging culture, which is influenced by postmodern philosophy, no longer assumes foundationalism as the primary standard of thought. As a result, many of the liberal-conservative battlegrounds, which were oppositional stances within

[46] J.R.R. Tolkien, *The Lord of the Rings: The Two Towers* (New York: Ballantine Books, 1966), 75.

a common foundational worldview, seem less significant or even irrelevant in the emerging culture.[47]

The decline of foundationalism will certainly remove some venom from the liberal-conservative divide. But challenges will abound in a new philosophical environment for the church. To be truly missional in the future, the church will need to be cautious about defending irrelevant or unhelpful issues and language. Theologian Stan Grenz comments that it would be ironic and tragic if Christians, after struggling for years to make sense of the great challenges of the modern world and modern philosophy (such as Darwinism, scientific criticism of the Bible, and the like) became the last defenders of dying modernity.[48]

In the wake of the horrors of World War I, the French military constructed the Maginot Line, a huge border fortress designed to protect France against invasion. The First World War was characterized by large, immobile armies battering each other with huge artillery pieces—and other terrible "modern" weapons—across static frontlines resulting in a horrific loss of life. By the time Nazi Germany invaded Belgium and France in 1940, the weapons of war had changed greatly. With huge technological developments in tanks and airplanes, armies became devastatingly mobile. The Germans simply went around the Maginot Line, passing through forests and other geography that was deemed impassible in previous wars. As the church moves into the emerging culture, it needs to find and deconstruct our current Maginot Lines.

Some of the issues generated by modern, foundational philosophy, which have defined the trench warfare between liberals and conservatives, will be part of this deconstruction. We evangelicals may also need to reconsider our own self-description. Evangelicalism was founded, in part, as a response to the lack of social concern and anti-intellectualism of fundamentalism.[49] The giants of the evangelical movement, such as Billy Graham, Harold Ockenga, Jim Rayburn, Bill Bright, Carl Henry, and many others, did much for the cause of Christ. Their legacy is secure. But in the last two

---

[47] Nancey Murphy, *Beyond Liberalism and Fundamentalism* (Harrisburg, Penn.: Trinity Press International, 1996). This excellent and important book demonstrates the liberal and conservative versions of foundationalism. It also offers great insight into how postmodern philosophy affects our theological positions and agenda.

[48] Stanley Grenz, *A Primer on Postmodernism* (Grand Rapids, Mich.: Wm. B. Eerdmans, 1996), 10.

[49] I believe you can see many of the roots of the emerging church in this adjustment and the later dialogue between liberals and conservatives over social action.

decades, the term *fundamentalist* has almost disappeared in its previous usage. We typically use this term now to denote militant, religious extremists. As a result, some of the characteristic critiques of fundamentalists—such as a lack of empathy, anti-intellectualism, divisiveness, and being culturally irrelevant—are invested in the term *evangelical*. Defending this term might be another Maginot Line for many Christians who have lovingly embraced this title.

In a new philosophical and cultural environment, the church has the wonderful opportunity to live in a reshaped orthodoxy. We have the chance to embrace and embody an expanded gospel (see chapter 2) that draws upon the best of the liberal and conservative traditions. There will be heresies, naive theologies, and lost values as we move into the future. And the postmodern philosophical environment and the many contours of the emerging culture will present new and previously unforeseen problems for the church. But at least we will have the opportunity to hear God's voice outside of the incriminations and ruts of the liberal-conservative debate.

A conversation of rapprochement between liberals and evangelicals has begun and is gaining momentum.[50] In *A Generous Orthodoxy*, Brian McLaren delves humbly and thoughtfully into the realities and dreams of a reshaped orthodoxy.[51] A reshaped orthodoxy does not mean we must jettison essentials of our faith, but it will mean challenging from the vantage point of a new perspective what we have previously deemed essential. Certainly, stands will be taken and divisions formed over new fault lines. The passion and mysteries of our faith and our human nature make this inevitable. But my sight is fixed on the possibilities for new friendships, collaborations, and mission in a season after we emerge from a long, cold war.

---

[50] To read in further detail, I recommend *The Nature of Confession: Evangelicals and Postliberals in Conversation*, edited by Timothy R. Phillips and Dennis L. Okholm (Downers Grove, Ill.: InterVarsity Press, 1996).

[51] Brian McLaren, *A Generous Orthodoxy* (Grand Rapids, Mich.: Zondervan, 2004). I am greatly indebted to Brian for his friendship and vision for theological and missional reconciliation.

FROM THOUGHT AND DIALOGUE TO PRACTICE

I love my dad dearly. What common sense I have comes from our endless conversations. Even our arguments, though peppered with my arrogance and adolescent insistence on always being right, have produced wonderful insights for both of us.

One of our arguments is infamous in Conder family lore. We were a strict, teetotaler Baptist family. As a child, I had been taught to expect all manner of ruin for those who drank alcohol. Then in college, I encountered peers who drank legally and moderately, and they were also mature followers of Jesus. So my dad and I got into a prolonged conversation on alcohol. Finally, totally exasperated at my dad's inflexibility on the issue, I asked him, "Dad, what would you do if Jesus showed up at the back door with a six-pack, and asked if he could come in and have a cold one with you?" Dad's reflexive answer was legendary. He said, "I'll just have to have faith that Jesus would never do that!" We both started laughing.

Dad's slip of the tongue seems relevant as we conclude this section on theological transitions of the church as it enters the emerging culture. Often we place our faith on our agenda for Jesus, rather than on the mysterious yet direct, complex yet simple Jesus whom we encounter in the Bible, the Christian community, and in our culture. So many of the fears I've highlighted in these chapters spring from allowing our fearful agendas to dictate the conversation between the church and the emerging culture. Thoughtful and challenging dialogue lies ahead for the existing and emerging church as we move into this new era. My hope is that we can move the conversation past our fears and oversimplifications and focus on Jesus' agenda for the church and society.

Of course, the journey of the church into the emerging culture is not just a transition of thought. It's also a transition in practice. In truth, our thoughts and practices should simultaneously inform each other. With this in mind, we move on to consider transitions in practice for the church in this era of change.

CHAPTER FIVE

Changing Your Worship Service: Why the Obvious Starting Place Is Usually Not the Best Starting Place!

The headline of a recent *New York Times* article on the emerging church proclaims, "Hip New Churches Pray to a Different Drummer."[52] The clear implication is that change in worship style is the key to emerging culture transition, so your church better get hip and hire a drummer real fast before this season passes you by.

It's understandable, though regrettable, that the conversation on the emerging church and postmodern transition often centers on changes in worship style. Many pastors mark their lives in seven-day frames between Sunday worship services. For pastors, these gatherings are extremely vulnerable performances where their vision, theology, and ministry skills are evaluated on a weekly basis by attendance and engagement. These services are also the flagships of the church community—the event most congregants care most about, a source of pride (or embarrassment), and the ultimate statement of identity for the fellowship. Changes in a church's worship service seem like the obvious place to begin a transition into emerging culture ministry.

But, in most cases, it's precisely the *wrong* starting point.

To illustrate this, let's take a quick look at three common scenarios that might lead a congregation to think that a change in its worship service is the answer to more effective ministry in the emerging culture. We'll see that each of them is likely to fail in its goal of transition—and may also yield a range of negative consequences.

SCENARIO 1: GENERATIONAL PANIC

The first situation occurs when the members of a congregation look at one another one Sunday and realize that certain age groups are missing—particularly young people. Over the past decade, churches everywhere have considered their makeup and have observed generational vacancies. A quick reaction is to develop a "postmodern worship service" to get the young people back!

[52] Title taken from *NYTimes.com* article, "Hip New Churches Pray to a Different Drummer" posted on February 18, 2004.

In 1985, the Chapel Hill Bible Church was quite a phenomenon in our community. A local newspaper had placed us on a top ten list of things that were "hot" in Chapel Hill—no small accomplishment for an evangelical church in a liberal college town! In our later service, seemingly every seat in our modest auditorium was filled with eager, note-taking students. The pastors in the high steeple churches on Franklin Street were dismayed that the whole church-going student population seemed to be making the longer walk past their churches to attend our services. Even five years later, when I arrived in 1990 to begin leading a small youth ministry, we had far more college students in our fellowship who were hoping to volunteer in this ministry than we had teens attending.

By 1995, our landscape had again changed dramatically. On Sundays, our parking lot looked like the sales lot for an auto dealer selling minivans. We had lots of young families, but the hundreds of college students who once attended our services were largely gone. Then, over the mid-semester break of 1995, approximately 100 students left our congregation en masse to attend a more popular, collegiate church. We were left with about 50 undergraduates and less than 30 persons in their twenties in the church.

After the mass exodus of students, our elders called an emergency retreat. We were deeply concerned that we were becoming a single-generation church by serving only our first boom of students (those who attended college in the 1970s and early '80s and were now moving through subsequent stages of life). We were in the early stages of building a new facility to continue ministering to the university community, and conversations about postmodernity and its potential ramifications for the church were progressing (though without a consensus) on our elder board.[53]

It would have been extremely easy to decide that the solution to our demographic dilemma was to start a nontraditional "postmodern worship service." But this move could have been a colossal mistake for us.

---

[53] Many churches and organizations were focused on Generation X ministries at this time. Through the leadership of Jimmy Long and others, we were already grappling with the importance of postmodern epistemology and culture for the future church.

We also could have radically changed our worship style at this time. This strategy would have required significant creation and re-direction of resources. It also would have been a capitulation to preference-based ministry—seeking to offer worship in the preferred style of a target audience. Yet such an effort would have been built around the false assumption that the group in question had a shared preference and that we could determine and then match that preference.

In our case, the large group of students who left us went to a church with a worship style that was much more traditional than our blended, quasi-contemporary music service. As is the case in most of such situations, the exodus of our youth had little or nothing to do with worship style. We could have spent a great deal of time, energy, and resources in seeking to change our service to what we thought those students wanted, without accomplishing our primary goal.

More significantly, this goal of wooing back the young often has little or nothing to do with postmodern transition. Granted, many have said that the generations born after the mid-1960s are the first postmodern generations in America. But this merely means that emerging culture perspectives are more highly represented among those who are under 40 years old. It says little or nothing about the preferences or values of the younger people in any specific community or church.

In the years since our church's emergency retreat, it has become clear that the emerging culture phenomenon is seeping into all ages and generations at uneven levels, depending upon the specifics of various local contexts. In our community, many of the churches and campus ministries that have thrived the most in their work with university students (undergraduates and graduates) and young adults have very little resemblance to emerging culture or postmodern ministries. Our particular community is filled with postmodern people, but most of them don't attend church—and I don't think they'd have attended the kind of worship service we could have started in 1995. Our fellowship simply lacked credibility and a voice with this population at that time. Changing our worship style would have done nothing to change that.

Generational demographics and the emerging culture transition are often two very different issues. The next scenario reveals some of the dangers and frustrations of intermingling these issues.

SCENARIO 2: A SERIES OF UNFORTUNATE CONFLICTS

A second scenario relates closely to the first. Again, the angst centers on the young and worship, but in this case the concern is that a congregation is failing to serve one of the generations within its own fellowship. It arises when there is a growing discontent within an existing church about its own worship style. In this situation, a shift to a more "postmodern style" (whatever that means!) can be looked at simultaneously as an answer to this angst and a progressive step forward in the church's ministry.

There is some legitimacy to this yearning. The presuppositions and appetites of the emerging culture are affecting all generations. There are many in our pews who yearn to see the values of mystery, narrative, spiritual holism, community, and spiritual experience worked into the idioms and forms of weekly worship services. In the last year, as our church started an emerging culture ministry initiative, we discovered that for decades many of our own members had been attending church politely and patiently, but they were waiting for these emerging culture passions to surface in the worship expression of our church.

But frustration about the worship service among the attendees in any particular church is almost always a multivariable train wreck of opinions, with allies of convenience and caricatured enemies. For some, the "postmodern interest" is mere subterfuge for their own preference for a certain style of music or for a parent's hope that a more contemporary worship service will make their teenager more willing to attend. Others justify their own desires for a more structured liturgical and sacramental service by pointing out that many persons with emerging culture predispositions are moving to churches with these more traditional styles. Just about every existing church has faced—on some level—a similar conflict over worship style during the last couple of decades.

I believe the real cause of this conflict is our culture of entitlement and the theological sanctification we give to our personal preferences. Our affluent, consumer-driven, multi-option society revolves around the market that provides outlets to suit our preferences. We feel a strong sense of entitlement and loyalty to these preferences. Computer platforms, grocery store chains, ethnic foods, and athletic teams become the subjects of passionate loyalty and debate. For church attendees, worship style can be just another place where we want to have it "our way."

As a former youth pastor, I still have nightmares about a group of teenagers trying to make a decision about what radio station or CD we'll listen to during a road trip. My head still hurts with memories of shouting, ultimatums, and shame-based negotiation. An innocent question like, "What kind of music do you want to hear?" served as an invitation to nuclear proliferation.

When it comes to worship, many congregations act like teens stuck in a van for a long trip. Church members embolden their preferences with memories of profound spiritual experiences and often a powerful sense of theological righteousness. An implicit demand that "what I believe" and "what I think about our world" should be reinforced at every worship gathering lurks behind most worship-style debates. Worship leaders experience this pull of diverse preferences on a weekly basis in many churches.

Worship style is neither an existing church issue nor an emerging church issue. It's an every church issue. As pastors and leaders, we work hard to demonstrate that the severity of these preferences stems from the entitlement of an entertainment-based society, rather than any biblical or spiritual mandate. But, if we're honest, we'll admit that we struggle to get that message across. In fact, most pastors struggle to keep our own personal preferences in appropriate balance when we're leading and designing worship gatherings.

Viewing these debates and conflicts as preference issues, rather than postmodern transition issues, is essential. As explained earlier, there are philosophies, principles, and values that inform the practice of emerging culture ministry. But there is no single emerging church or "postmodern" worship style.

At the Chapel Hill Bible Church, we've had the unfortunate experience of letting issues of worship preference and emerging culture transition become intermingled. Our worship style has changed significantly over the past three decades. In the 1980s, our style was predominantly a contemplative, acoustic style with some movement toward mainstream Christian rock. With new leadership in the following decade, we shifted toward a blended style that added classical music, choral pieces, and traditional hymns to some remaining contemporary elements. The significant shifts in worship style (and leadership style) left a residue of dissatisfaction and fearful distrust in our congregation. Some members felt their preferences had been ignored during this transition; others feared that the style of music they loved might be lost in a future transition. In 2000, the resignation of one of our primary worship leaders reopened the conversation about musical style and genres in our worship services. Within a year, our music style had changed again—this time, to a much more upbeat, contemporary style. The musical changes were accompanied by significant changes in the tone of the service and other primary idioms of worship.

Sadly, our momentum toward an emerging culture ministry initiative picked up during this same time frame. Despite relentless efforts on our part, it was nearly impossible to separate the discussion of the values and goals of our emerging culture ministry from the angst and angry dialogue about worship styles. As we've seen in previous chapters, the theological presuppositions of the emerging culture are already subject to strong fears and inappropriate oversimplifications. In our case, these same fears were being accentuated and even enflamed by powerful prejudices and preferences regarding worship styles.

We descended into a series of unfortunate and unnecessary conflicts and conversations that strayed far from the goals, hopes, and realities of emerging culture ministry. Many regrettable and hurtful comments were made in public forums. Accusations were made about the agenda of younger church attendees, and whole genres of artistic expression were rejected in sweeping dismissals. A painful legacy remains from this time of conflict.

So many fellowships that thought of postmodern transition as a "worship style phenomenon" have begun in this place and suffered great consequences. The residuals have included irreconcilable staff conflicts, the formation of rival and competitive congregations, confused church members who feel the pain of these disagreements without understanding the substance of the differences, and—once again—a church whose mission in society is dulled by the inward and selfish direction of its energies.

Tragically, the emphasis on worship style often leads us far away from the soul of emerging culture transitions. Our final scenario elaborates on this statement and begins to crack open the door of understanding to the practices of ministry transition.

SCENARIO 3: THE GOSPEL AS PERFORMANCE, MOMENT, OR EVENT

It's well past midnight and the crowd has headed home. The speaker has long since returned to the hotel, and the band finally finished the load-out and their bus is now driving off into the night toward their next event. As the evening draws to a close, you feel the intense satisfaction of having hosted a well-received event—or maybe the seething embarrassment of a disappointing show. You also sense the approach of the inevitable wave of exhaustion that follows in the wake of these many weeks of promoting the event, recruiting and managing volunteers, supervising technical logistics, and accommodating the personal needs and requests of the performers. Soon you will face the question that arises after every big event: *Was it really worth it? Will the lasting impact justify the immense effort required to create the event?*

Most pastors and church leaders have stood in these shoes before. Some pastors experience these same questions in the wake of each weekly worship service. *Was it worth the effort? Was this the best use of our energy?*

A few years ago, I was at an Emergent meeting and casually mentioned that I'd spent more than 30 hours preparing the previous week's sermon. Doug Pagitt, a friend and colleague, raised a challenging eyebrow at this time expenditure. My justification was that preaching to a congregation of Ph.D.'s and graduate students demands arduous preparation. Pagitt shot back, "Wouldn't the world be better off if you spent two hours working on the sermon and the rest of the week feeding the hungry in your community?" Now I often repeat this challenge as a mantra when I begin writing sermons or seminars.

This is not intended as an attack on big, church-based events, well-prepared sermons, or intricate intentionality in crafting worship experiences. But we in the church do run the risk of encapsulating the gospel or God's kingdom into a performance, moment, or event in our attempts to compete for attention with the myriad of events in our omnipresent media. We live in the wake of an information-entertainment culture that reduces the world to sound bites and 30-second commercials. It even turns horrific disasters into media events. This creates a great appetite for entertainment, as well as a temptation for the church to think that the best way (the only way?) to proclaim its message is through well-crafted, high-profile events.

In its essence the gospel is not a moment, event, or performance. Better events and new worship styles are not the answer. Our pluralistic, postmodern, and post-Christian culture is not only event-savvy; I believe it's largely weary of Christian events. This culture doesn't need churches that major in offering the right kind of worship service or performance event. What this culture desperately needs to see is God's story and kingdom as morally good, plausible, and embodied in communities.

The church landscape is indeed filled with "hip new churches praying to a different drummer." Yet the reduction of the emerging culture transition into a search for the right programmatic worship formula (in order to reach new generations) not only obscures the essence of this transition, but also challenges and even contradicts the breadth and scope of God's story and his plans for this world.

Throughout the remaining chapters, I will continue to stress that transition often has little to do with stylistic and programmatic changes. Instead, the shift to emerging culture ministry requires changes in the definition and mindset of the most elemental expressions of Christian community—spiritual formation, leadership, community formation, and mission. Once we explore the necessary shifts in each of these four areas, we'll return to the subject of worship. And in the process of our examination, it will become obvious that the church's transition into the emerging culture also involves a fundamental shift in our definition and expression of worship.

CHAPTER SIX

Transition in Spiritual Formation

One of the great privileges of being a pastor is that I'm invited into refreshingly honest conversations about the spiritual lives of those in our community. In the midst of these conversations, I've found that many of the people I most admire for their deep and vital spiritual lives often complain of spiritual dormancy and frustration. To illustrate this, let me offer quick profiles of four long-time friends who speak often of their own spiritual inadequacy and failure, yet whose lives seem marked by the authentic presence of God's spirit.

One friend has strong and often angry questions about some elements of Christian theology and some of the norms of church life. He struggles to practice any regular discipline of Bible study and prayer. Yet his life is marked by deep connections to Christian community, a relentless kindness to a vast array of neighbors of differing beliefs and lifestyles, and a remarkable wisdom about pursuing the purposes of God in our community.

Another friend feels a strong sense of shame about his sexual decisions, as well as his inability to sustain a career path toward professional ministry. Nonetheless, he maintains a tremendous openness to God's presence in his life.

A third friend is extremely angry with God and her Christian community. She is homosexual and has chosen a celibate lifestyle. She wishes she were heterosexual, and longs to be married and have children. She has prayed continually for these life changes; but her orientation is unchanged, which has led to great anger and frustration. Yet she has a wonderful understanding of Christian community and creates remarkable prayers and artwork that express the character of God and the journey of faith.

A fourth friend would never even call herself a Christian. But her care for my family and her spiritual wisdom exceeds that of so many self-professed "mature Christians."

The faith journeys of these friends, and many others like them, challenge many of the assumed notions of spiritual formation and spiritual maturity in Christian communities. Some of our expectations about spiritual development seem flawed or even dishonest. Others appear sound, but are overexpressed and overgeneralized. If the church seeks to speak with authenticity to the spiritual longings and needs of postmodern people, I believe we need to free ourselves from false expectations about spiritual formation.

CHALLENGING COMMON ASSUMPTIONS ABOUT SPIRITUAL FORMATION

For years the church tended to think of spiritual formation as a one-way journey toward greater certainty about matters of faith. But embedded in such a modern definition are a number of assumptions that are increasingly called into question by a postmodern worldview.

Assumption 1: Spiritual Growth Is Linear

First, the belief that spiritual formation is linear and measurable needs to be questioned. A modern worldview built around the scientific method and propositional truth reinforces the burdensome assumption that one can measure spirituality and consistently discern gradations of spiritual maturity. Assuming spirituality to be linear can also place an inordinate amount of attention on specific personal sins. In this mindset, certain sins are deemed so heinous that they interrupt the linear progression of spiritual growth and take the sinner back to square one. As a result, we think it necessary to create not only gradations in spiritual maturity but also in sin—making a false distinction between "misdemeanors" that can be worked through and "felonies" that take us back to a beginning point (or place intense pressure on the need for a dramatic conversion or liberation experience that allows freedom from the felonies).

Openness to the emerging culture perspective on the subjectivity of experience reminds us that the spiritual life is not always linear. Spiritual journeys are filled with strange and surprising turns—failures that are redemptively shaped into convictions and wisdom, and arduous efforts that bear no apparent fruit. The Bible offers numerous narratives and raw poetic expressions concerning men and women who followed God's lead without being aware of God's presence. These literal and figurative desert experiences are sometimes lost in our descriptions of the Christian path.

Assumption 2: Spiritual Development Leads to Greater Certainty

A postmodern penchant for mystery also challenges some of the certainties we impose on the spiritual life. Much of our spiritual education is designed to remove uncertainty. But the faith journeys of God's people are filled with long—and not always successful— searches for God's will, a good measure of confusion, and many times a reduction of their certainties. Even as my relationship with God has deepened over the years, I find I am less certain about matters of faith and belief than I once was. I've found that honesty with my preadolescent children often requires that I reply, "I don't know," to many of their questions about God.

Assumption 3: Spiritual Development Means Life Will Improve

We must also reexamine how the optimism of U.S. culture has shaped our faith expectations. Technology and innovation will solve our problems. Education will abolish injustice. Progress is inevitable, and our lives will generally improve with time. We pass this optimism on in our theology. Those who walk with God will experience better lives. We use implicitly optimistic terms like "spiritual growth" to denote the journey of faith.

But this isn't always honest. In fact, our implicit promises of spiritual betterment often seem highly irrelevant in this age. Those who follow in the path of Christ often do so in difficult circumstances; faithful people experience pain and hardship. The emerging culture witnesses the harsh realities of an age confronting global terrorism, a growing polarization between the wealthiest and the most poor, and environmental deterioration. Natural disasters and the harshest realities of human greed and injustice are graphically depicted and disseminated in our media.

Pastor Craig Barnes explains that the myth of betterment demands a Christian subculture that is isolated from reality and holds unrealistic expectations for Christian leaders:

> The advice peddlers assure us that Christian principles will offer greater success in these areas of struggle. Yet the truth is that our formulas don't work a whole lot better than those of the world. That is what makes the subculture—and its isolation from reality—necessary...When church leaders betray the marks of human character, or worse yet, succumb to temptation, their failure undermines our ability to believe and sell the myth that Christians have found the secret to fulfillment. The real difficultly we have with these leaders is not that they sinned, but that they have betrayed our dream.[54]

The emerging culture is poised to indict even the unintended dishonesty of some of our promises for a better life as we follow the path of Christ.

Assumption 4: Spiritual Development Is Individualistic

Our description of spirituality can also be exceedingly individualistic. Community may be described as important—but often it's viewed only as a tool to improve personal spirituality. As I've noted earlier, many in the emerging culture experience a powerful spiritual connectedness in their community and primary relationships. This calls the church to be more sensitive to the spiritual nature of community. What does talk of personal salvation and a personal relationship with God mean for our experience of community? Do our churches have words for communities, associations, and even

---

[54] Craig Barnes, *Yearning: Living Between How It Is and How It Ought to Be* (Downers Grove, Ill.: InterVarsity Press, 1992), 22-23.

nations? Something feels intuitively wrong in the individualism of our theology and spiritual nurture.

Assumption 5: Spiritual Development Means Increased Knowledge of God

Our expectations and methods of spiritual care are often exceedingly cognitive with a near obsession for understanding. For many churches, spiritual training is regularly reduced to the transfer of information. One impediment to our church's development of an emerging culture ministry has been an insistence on understanding. We tend to think we cannot affirm or endorse potential mission without clear definitions, measurable outcomes, and clarity.

To many in the emerging culture, this strong emphasis on understanding and the reduction of spirituality to the cognitive seems overblown. Postmodern people have become more comfortable in trafficking in the unexplainable. Although contemporary science continually strives for progress, we expect a mixed bag from most scientific innovations. The emerging culture regularly hears the scientific community affirm the realities of chaos that cannot be placed in order, formulas that cannot be applied universally, and mysteries that cannot be unraveled. Some of what emerging culture persons "know" or believe has been derived from non-cognitive sources such as intuition, community experiences, and random events. A cognitive approach and expectations of significant clarity to something as ethereal and subjective as spirituality seems ill-suited.

In all this, I am not suggesting there is no truth to be found in modern understandings of spiritual formation. Our spiritual journeys should be marked by hope and optimism. Our experience and knowledge of God and God's kingdom create and shape hope. There will always be a cognitive element of spiritual formation. Nonetheless, the emerging culture demands that we change our emphasis, expectations, and presuppositions regarding spiritual formation.

SPIRITUAL FORMATION AS RHYTHM, RULE, AND PRACTICE

The advent of the emerging culture is causing a reformation—perhaps even a revolution—in the church's understanding of spiritual formation. Instead of a compartmentalized spirituality that focuses on personal choices, we are seeing the growth of a new approach to spiritual formation that emphasizes a rule of life and rhythms of spiritual practices drawing from a vast array of Christian traditions.

Authors like Richard Foster, Brian McLaren, and Tony Jones have all made important contributions to this transformation. Building on his long-time emphasis on contemplative spirituality, Richard Foster, in *Streams of Living Water*, affirms the many streams of Christian spirituality.[55] Brian McLaren, in *A Generous Orthodoxy*, affirms seven distinct conceptualizations of the person and ministry of Jesus to confer the dignity and importance to various Christian traditions.[56] Tony Jones's *The Sacred Way* describes the many spiritual practices developed and refined throughout Christian history, showing how divergent traditions can be applied to the mission of spiritual nurture in the church.[57]

Thankfully, there is a widening pool of resources to aid churches, Christians, and spiritual sojourners in the exploration of spiritual practices that support this transformation of orientation. It's truly exciting to see churches making use of a wide range of historic and experiential spiritual practices, such as labyrinths, body prayers, praying the hours, meditation using the repetition of historical prayers and liturgies like the Jesus Prayer, *lectio divina*, the integration of art and physical practices into prayer, fasting, the use of contemporary and historical symbols and icons, and the restoration and veneration of the Eucharist and baptism in traditions that once minimized these rites.

[55] I recently marveled at a Richard Foster event that our church hosted. The long list of sponsors cut across the classic divisions of Christian traditions in our community. The classic trench lines of Catholic/Protestant and liberal/conservative are certainly eroding in our community. The volume of interest and attendance also affirms the breadth of the change in common thought on spiritual formation. See Richard Foster, *Streams of Living Water: Celebrating the Great Traditions of Christian Faith* (San Francisco: HarperSanFrancisco, 1998).

[56] Brian McLaren, *A Generous Orthodoxy* (Grand Rapids, Mich.: Zondervan, 2003).

[57] Tony Jones, *The Sacred Way* (Grand Rapids, Mich.: Zondervan, 2004).

But just as a simple change in worship style won't automatically help our churches better respond to the postmodern culture, these rich spiritual experiences can become barriers to renewal if they are simply tacked on to an old understanding of spiritual development. To facilitate a real and lasting transition in our spiritual formation, we need new organizing disciplines to frame these spiritual practices. I believe that perhaps the most critical discipline to affirm in the emerging culture is the practice of hospitality.

HOSPITALITY AS A SPIRITUAL DISCIPLINE

Although I grew up in a community and a church that habitually practiced hospitality, I never considered the spiritual intricacies of hospitality before. In fact, I'm embarrassed to admit that I thought of hospitality as the fallback contribution for those who could not exercise serious spiritual gifts like leadership, teaching, or organization. But when I started out in professional ministry, I discovered quickly that team building and community building would be among my most significant tasks. Although business and management books were becoming common fare for pastors, I'm grateful that some wise friends guided me to the writings of Henri Nouwen. As I plunged in, I was surprised to hear Nouwen describe hospitality as a spiritual discipline.[58] Now after years spent contemplating this idea, I have difficulty overstating the significance of hospitality in the spiritual mission of the church.[59]

In *Reaching Out*, Nouwen paints the spiritual movement from hostility to hospitality as an essential reflex and result of the spiritual life. Nouwen sees hospitality as being characterized by great expectation for the presence of God in his relational encounters. For Nouwen, hospitality is a combination of receptivity, openness to others, and honesty. He writes, "Hospitality wants to offer friendship without binding the guest [Receptivity] and freedom without leaving him alone [Honesty]."[60] Elaborating on this simple definition, Nouwen writes:

---

[58] Maybe hospitality was an act of kindness but never something as serious as a discipline! Of course, over time I also learned that kindness is an essential spiritual discipline.

[59] Having had the privilege to travel in many different cultures, I realize how ridiculous and obvious this statement is in many cultures outside of the United States.

[60] Henri Nouwen, *Reaching Out* (New York: Doubleday, 1975), 71.

Hospitality, therefore, means primarily the creation of a free space where the stranger can enter and become a friend instead of an enemy. Hospitality is not to change people, but to offer them space where change can take place. It is not to bring men and women over to our side, but to offer freedom not disturbed by dividing lines. It is not to lead our neighbor into a corner where there are no alternatives left...It is not an educated intimidation with good books, good stories and good works, but the liberation of fearful hearts so that words can find roots and bear ample fruit...The paradox of hospitality is that it wants to create emptiness, not a fearful emptiness, but a friendly emptiness where strangers can enter and discover themselves as created free; free to sing their own songs, speak their own languages, dance their own dances; free also to leave...Hospitality is not the subtle invitation to adopt the life style of the host, but the gift of a chance for the guest to find his own...Reaching out to others without being receptive to them is more harmful than helpful and easily leads to manipulation and even to violence, violence in thoughts, words, and actions.[61]

To practice receptivity of this magnitude requires honesty. Nouwen continues:

Real receptivity asks for confrontation, because space can only be a welcoming space when there are clear boundaries...We are not hospitable when we leave our house to strangers and let them use it any way they want...When we want to be really hospitable we not only have to receive strangers but also to confront them by an unambiguous presence, not hiding ourselves behind neutrality but showing our ideas, opinions, and life style clearly and distinctly. No real dialogue is possible between somebody and a nobody. We can enter into communication with the other only when our life choices, attitudes and viewpoints offer the boundaries that challenge strangers to become aware of their own position and to explore it critically.[62]

[61] Nouwen, 71-72, 97-98.
[62] Nouwen, 98-99.

A community commitment to the receptivity and honesty that Nouwen bundles into his invitation to hospitality would catalyze an enormous transformation in the authenticity, accessibility, and mission of the church.

Pervasive hospitality is necessary to initiate a needed inclusivity in our ministries of spiritual formation. Much of the church's failure in spiritual formation is related to the perception from both insiders and outsiders that the church is reflexively exclusive or judgmental. I see this perception when I meet with people from outside our church who've been referred to me because of some spiritual concern or life issue. These guests typically approach the meeting with emotions ranging from defensive nervousness to abject fear. But I also see some of these same apprehensions in Christians who make an appointment to discuss a failing marriage, their sexual orientation, an addiction, or some other "forbidden" circumstance or sin. They've been trained to expect that their pain and confession will yield some level of exclusion. Thus, our inability to practice the receptivity that Nouwen recommends ultimately prevents those opportunities where we can honestly describe God's graciousness, love, and concern for our broken lives.

One could argue that the church's ministry of spiritual formation begins with hospitality in any culture and era. But in the emerging culture, which experiences spirituality primarily in community and often needs to belong before believing, a commitment to the discipline of hospitality is urgently necessary.

The discipline of hospitality opens the possibility for spiritual formation and provides it with drive and direction. Let's take a look at four interrelated facets of hospitality, each of which is critical for spiritual formation in the emerging culture.

Divine Hospitality: Welcoming God's Presence in Our Midst

While we may tend to think of hospitality primarily in terms of our relationships with one another, the spiritual practice of hospitality begins with our openness to God. The One who created each of us longs to walk alongside us as well. The practice of divine hospitality includes receptivity to God's voice and presence, and honesty in our prayerful communication with God.

The Psalms offer a musical and poetic demonstration of divine hospitality. Consider the rawness of need expressed in these verses from Psalm 88:1-5:

> O Lord, the God who saves me,
> day and night I cry out before you.
> May my prayer come before you;
> turn your ear to my cry.
> For my soul is full of trouble
> and my life draws near the grave.
> I am counted among those who go down to the pit;
> I am like a man without strength.
> I am set apart with the dead,
> like the slain who lie in the grave,
> whom you remember no more,
> who are cut off from your care.

The uncensored honesty and desperate receptivity to God that we find in these verses offer us a freedom to practice a similar hospitality toward God with a variety of emotional tenors.

The historical spiritual practices that are being rediscovered throughout many portions of the church can be framed and used as acts of divine hospitality. They are not talismans or models to be programmatically instituted to ensure spiritual formation. Instead, these practices—like the prayers of the Psalms—are guides to divine hospitality, which model a posture of sensitivity to the God who is graciously present in our lives.

Communicational Hospitality: Fostering Dialogue

We can become hospitable in our communication, if we can relearn the skill of dialogue. Conversation is becoming a lost art. For all the communication possibilities in our culture, we are losing the ability to speak and listen to one another. Whether we are politically conservative or liberal, we don't trust the media. We believe we must use news sources that reflect our political viewpoints in order to get the truth.

Living in a community where the local newspaper serves three major universities, I often hear sports fans from each college complain that the newspaper is inadequate or unfair in its coverage of their team. Many of these fans will tell you that fair and accurate information can be found only on the Web sites and publications associated with their particular team. In a fluid and preference-driven culture that offers so many options for information, we have both the capability and the proclivity to spend most of our time among those who affirm our viewpoints. We are losing the ability to talk with those who disagree with us.

Henri Nouwen has shown how receptivity and honesty are the root activities of real dialogue—hospitality applied to our conversations. This practice of communicational hospitality would liberate the voice of the church in a community-craved culture that typically hears only the voices of preference, favoritism, prejudice, and judgment.

Relational Hospitality: Practicing Kindness

Relational hospitality—a commitment to receptivity, honesty, and kindness in our relational and social lives—is also necessary. Living in a university environment, the consistent practice of kindness has been a persistent challenge for us. In our community we value critique, analysis, and ideological jousting above all other skills. The worst fate for an academic endeavor is apathy. Important ideas provoke reaction and criticism, scrutiny of the data, and replication of one's method. Though this is accentuated in a university-dominated community, the myth of truly objective critique and analysis that exists outside relationship is a product of the modern worldview. As the church begins to reformulate itself in light of the subjectivity and relational intensity of the emerging culture, we need to encourage a rule of kindness that trumps our inclinations to critique and compete.

Miles Reck is a remarkable man who has committed to a rule of kindness as a discipline of relational hospitality. He graces our worship gatherings with a weekly walk of prayerful intercession. He graces our cluttered and sometimes mournful lives with amazing cookies that he makes as a ritual of prayer for those in need. Over many years of intense experimentation, Miles has created and perfected five different cookie recipes, all named for missional inspirations in our community. The cookies are made at great personal cost and consistently appear as a gift of encouragement and a mark of prayer to those in our community who are celebrating as well as those who are weary or mournful. Miles arrived at our door at a time when my wife and I were deeply fatigued with the demands of ministry and a family health crisis. We nearly wept as he shared the prayer and love that were primary ingredients in the cookies he delivered to us. Every time we eat these cookies or share them with friends, we taste the kindness of his relational hospitality.

Theological reflection can also invigorate a rule of relational hospitality and a practice of kindness. I was recently having dinner with Dan Allender, an author and president of Mars Hill Graduate School, who also offers up kindness and hospitality on huge platters. In a conversation that drifted toward theology, Dan described himself, at the bare minimum, as a "one-point Calvinist." He believes uncompromisingly in sin, the depravity of humanity, and the presence of sinful brokenness in our world. Although sin and alienation from God drive humanity to violence, self-protection, and all acts of unkindness, Dan explained that a theology of sin could motivate a liberating kindness. Aware of our sinfulness, we can be liberated from inappropriate competition (since we are all broken) and be free to offer kindness to each other. By acknowledging our own sin, we can be liberated from self-protection fueled by shame and can extend ourselves in vulnerability and kindness to one another. Awareness of the depth of our sinfulness can strengthen our connection to those around us and eradicate the self-righteousness, entitlements, and fears that prevent relational hospitality.

Cultural Hospitality: Welcoming Strangers and Exiles

A final form of hospitality, requiring immense resuscitation in many congregations, is cultural hospitality. Enlightenment thinking has created hard separations between the secular and the sacred or spiritual. The modern era's demand that the church justify its belief systems against the assumed objectivity of the scientific method has led to suspicion and entrenched battle between church and culture. Hundreds of years of cultural dominance by Christianity have led the church to an attitude of entitlement that fully expects all of culture to adopt and respect our belief systems. This combination of forces has led the church to an embattled unkindness toward contemporary culture. In an emerging culture that values diversity and deemphasizes sacred-secular boundaries, the church's desire to invite society into spiritual community has been muted. Cultural hospitality means an intentional kindness to our surrounding culture.

There are many scriptural imperatives that should drive us to this kindness, confront our aggressive entitlement, and diminish our idealistic expectations of cultural conflict. In Peter's manifesto of mission in 1 Peter 2:11-12, we are urged to a lifestyle of hospitality, goodness, and kindness:

> Dear friends, I urge you, as aliens and strangers in the world, to abstain from sinful desires, which war against your soul. Live such good lives among the pagans that, though they accuse you of doing wrong, they may see your good deeds and glorify God on the day he visits us.

This text reminds us that we are to live as kind and nonviolent aliens who embody a present and coming kingdom that differs greatly from the norms of our society.

In *Resident Aliens*, Stanley Hauerwas and Will Willimon write persuasively that the church's call is to form an authentic community that, while not dictated by the nonbiblical and kingdom-averse assumptions of our culture, serves as a community of blessing to this culture.[63] Old Testament scholar Walter Brueggemann has shown that the theme of exile is one of the dominant organizing motifs of the Scriptures. God calls us to accept our status as an exilic people and to live in journey toward our kingdom home.[64]

These leaders remind us that cultural hospitality is more than acknowledgement of status and eternal sojourners in exile. Cultural hospitality is an essential posture of mission. In his brilliant commentary on 1 Corinthians, Gordon Fee demonstrates the missional imperatives of cultural hospitality in his analysis of 1 Corinthians 8:1–11:1. Fee persuasively argues that the caution to the Corinthian church about eating meat offered to idols is more specifically a prohibition from participating in the idolatrous and promiscuous temple life of this culture. Paul uses unequivocal terms of scandal, spiritual destruction, and demonic participation to make this point. (See 1 Corinthians 8:11, 10:21.) But when the scene changes to questions about eating meat in private homes (1 Corinthians 10:23–11:1), Paul's tone changes markedly to one of conscience and sensitivity. Here, his advice to eat or not eat is based on sensitivity to one's host or company.

Christians have long misinterpreted these verses as guides to avoid offending other Christians with grey-area moral decisions. But the biblical context is far more concerned with Christian sensitivity to pagans and those outside of the church in Corinth. The driving point of this final paragraph is a cultural hospitality driven by mission. Sensitivity to the concerns of our surrounding culture—listening to their questions and objections—is a vital act of mission.[65]

---

[63] Stanley Hauerwas and William H. Willimon, *Resident Aliens: Life in the Christian Colony* (Nashville: Abingdon Press, 1989).

[64] See Walter Brueggemann, *Cadences of Home: Preaching Among Exiles* (Louisville, Ky.: Westminster John Knox Press, 1997), and *Ichabod Toward Home: The Journey of God's Glory* (Grand Rapids, Mich.: Wm. B. Eerdmans, 2002).

In the harsh secularism and bitter intellectual challenges of Christianity in modernity, the church has lost its theology of general revelation that teaches of the presence of God's voice throughout society and creation. We've also forgotten to exemplify God's love and redemptive intention for the whole of creation through pervasive kindness, sensitivity, and hospitality to the culture that surrounds us. Our acknowledgement of our status as exiles, as well as being agents of God's kingdom in a creation he dearly loves, does not allow for an entitled bitterness in our interaction with society. The great biblical narratives of kindness and receptivity to strangers portray the instinctive invitations of hospitality from a people who acknowledge their own exile and their privilege as agents in the formation of God's redemptive kingdom.

PREACHING AS A MINISTRY OF KINDNESS AND INTIMACY

The transition called for in our spiritual formation is not so much an overhaul of methods as it is a change (or rediscovery) of rhythm, rule, and practice, and the pervasive applications of disciplines such as hospitality and kindness. But these evolutions of rule and discipline will certainly transform traditional expressions of ministry. Let's take a look at how they might shape two areas: preaching and programming.

To minister effectively in the emerging culture, I believe our preaching must become an intentional expression of intimacy and kindness. The pulpits of our churches have long been vehicles for biblical exposition, spiritual encouragement, motivation, cultural and political awareness, and ministry vision—and these functions will certainly continue in the future. Yet many sermons are marked by tones of cultural despair (in contrast to heavenly hopes), militancy, absolute certainty, moral judgment, and anger. When these tones are present, disciplines like hospitality and kindness are contradicted and discouraged.

---

[65] Gordon Fee, *The First Epistle to the Corinthians (The New International Commentary on the New Testament)* (Grand Rapids, Mich.: Wm. B. Eerdmans, 1987), 357-491. See especially pages 483-491. There is great irony in the reading of this text. So often these directives by Paul have been used to curtail missional activities or risks because of offense within the church. I believe they challenge us to do the opposite—to prevent church sensitivities from hindering acts of missional kindness and hospitality.

Even when the tone of our sermons is generous, the traditional preparation and delivery of a sermon by a single voice implicitly reinforces spiritual transformation as individualistic and compartmentalized to specific events (in this case a speech event). Sermons that are filled with information and analysis affirm that spiritual formation is highly cognitive (receiving information and understanding) and that we can expect spiritual maturity to progress in relationship to the amount of information we take in.

These are certainly strong generalizations. Most of the preachers I know already display sensitivity to the potential downfalls of these methods, tones, and content-driven styles. Emerging culture passions—such as narrative, dialogical preaching, and artistic expression—are quickly infiltrating our pulpits. I applaud these changes, especially when they are an extension of our theological and biblical reflection, rather than an effort to entertain a changed culture. When these elements are not present, we run the risk of falling back into all the oversimplified dialogues and ministry mistakes we examined earlier in the book (such as devaluing the Bible as simply proposition or moralism, or seeing the gospel as disconnected from culture).

But our preaching can go further. Our preaching can model and energize spiritual formation that is marked by disciplines of hospitality and kindness. I've been privileged to observe and learn this from many talented friends. Brian McLaren, a leading voice in the emerging church, models kindness and invitation in his preaching. Even when speaking in antagonistic environments, Brian consistently models the hospitality of an invitation to safe places. Doug Pagitt, of the Solomon's Porch community in Minneapolis, is another leader who is uniquely gifted in this practice. Pagitt invites the community to participate in the preparation, delivery, and evaluation of the preaching. The tone and trajectory of each week's sermon is shaped by a weekly dialogue that has preceded it. The delivery of the sermon reflects this conversation and then invites further dialogue. It becomes a sermon of many voices. At Solomon's Porch, preaching is not just an extension of community; it's an expression of community.

Tim Keel, the founding pastor of Jacob's Well in Kansas City, Missouri, has taught me volumes about preaching as a ministry of intimacy, hospitality, and kindness. Tim's sermons avoid the common pitfalls of stopping with information transfer, sentimentality, and the reduction of the Christian life to simplistic promises. He leaves room for mystery and creative response to God's inspired Word. His sermons arise from his intimate connection with this community. Words of deep personal vulnerability and weakness accompany his humor and insight. His sermons are the kind words of a gentle leader who invites dear friends into an honest, hopeful, and mystical embrace with a triune God.

As one of Tim's sermons concludes at Jacob's Well, you can feel the congregation eagerly anticipating the celebration of the Eucharist. Then, after receiving the elements at the front of the church, congregants reform themselves by holding hands or placing arms over one another's shoulders and forming long lines that erase the center aisle as they sing with contagious joy and enthusiasm. It's truly one of the most joyful celebrations of the Eucharist I've been privileged to join. The joy of this celebration is a natural response to Tim's intimate exercise of kindness in the pulpit.

CREATING SPACE: PROGRAMMING FOR HOSPITALITY

Over the past 20 years, I've sat in countless meetings where a great idea was squashed due to lack of space—be it physical space in the church building or relational space within the community. This is a common story for so many churches. We've become more than seven-days-a-week churches, we've become 24/7 traffic jams of frenetic activity. This should be celebrated—many of the programs that fill church communities and their buildings are outstanding. But pastors and leaders confront many difficult decisions about programming and the use of space. Although there is no perfect formula for these decisions, I'd like to offer a recommendation: What if we made our program decisions based primarily on how well they embody the kind of hospitality that enhances spiritual formation?

Such a focus would raise two key questions about our current and potential programming. The first concerns our level of activity. Does our level of programming create expectations of busyness that prevent our community members from living hospitable lives? Most fellowships are sensitive to this question. Nonetheless, the value of being busy can be communicated subtly in our gatherings. Even if we preach about the need for boundaries, when our announcements and newsletters are filled with programming needs, we implicitly reinforce the value of busyness.

The second question concerns the nature of our programs. What percentage of our efforts serves only the members of our congregation instead of inviting the greater community to benefit from our resources? "Insider" events that require huge amounts of energy, time, and finances can easily become beloved traditions that so dominate our landscape that they preclude opportunities for hospitality. A similar question would involve the level of support a congregation gives to wider Christian events at the exclusion of community events.

I've been fortunate to serve in a fellowship with a historic commitment to creating space for our community, and I've witnessed the tremendous missional results of this commitment. For three decades, we were the only sizable, public facility in an event-rich university community that didn't charge rent. This generosity, when combined with a missional commitment to lean toward minimal programming while welcoming outside groups with a wide range of social and political values (within boundaries of propriety), created a "perfect storm" of hospitality and mission. Through the years our building was filled with groups from our community. Liberal animal-rights groups met in the next office over from conservative political gatherings. Countless children and youth who grew up in Chapel Hill have memories of music recitals and family receptions in our building. When our congregation was forced to move off campus, due to space and parking concerns, a community that is normally resistant to growth (and church growth) stood up in droves to lobby the town council to approve our new facility. The new facility was already viewed as community space.

I've watched, sometimes in awe, as this commitment to hospitality has bred more radical decisions. In order to maintain the freedom and resources to continue our mission of keeping our space available to community groups like the North Carolina Symphony, we've had to deny several requests to host high-profile Christian events that would have ministered only to the Christian subculture. When we were building our new facility on a very tight budget, an outstanding Christian private school made a very tempting offer to fund other phases of our building campaign if they could share our facility as their home. But we were concerned that having a private school on site might disenfranchise those with lower incomes in our fellowship or might lead to a situation where the children, youth, and families who were a part of the school would feel a sense of ownership of the space that was not extended to the wider community.

Creating space for others and programmatic hospitality are reflexes of our fellowship. These commitments have probably done more to communicate our mission to the wider community than anything else we've accomplished.

SPIRITUAL FORMATION: AN INVITATION TO A WAY OF LIFE

I was sitting in a local pub with a group of people from our church, when a friend of one person in our party walked up. We were deep in the throes of a weekly theological conversation, and this newcomer (an admitted non-churchgoer) was delighted to buy a round for the group and join in our dialogue. His thoughts and critiques were welcomed and encouraged. After several evenings like this, he was eager to become involved in our community. Our invitation to him was not to accept a doctrinal position or body of knowledge, to adopt the optimistic promise of a better life, to improve his spirituality, or to rest in clarity. The invitation was to join a community marked by a way of life founded upon hospitality, kindness, and the path of Jesus.

Similar stories are happening in many other Christian communities as well. In an emerging culture marked by a deep yearning for relationship, greater comfort with ambiguity, and a longing for embodied beliefs, the church's mission of spiritual formation must change dramatically. We must revitalize disciplines like hospitality, dialogue, and kindness, and allow these practices to frame our spiritual development and ministry decisions.

Transition in Leadership

When I think of the primary metaphors that influenced my earlier understandings of church leadership, three quickly come to mind—the teacher, the CEO, and the therapist.

During my time in seminary, the primary metaphor for pastoral leadership was the classroom, with the pastor as teacher. Our seminary curriculum called for learning the intricate skills of biblical exegesis and the craft of homiletics. The persistent image was the scholar/pastor who retreated to a study for diligent prayer and reflection, academic analysis of a biblical text, and intense preparation. We accepted the standard that every minute preaching demanded an hour of study and preparation. The primary expression of leadership occurred in sermons, as fruits of our preparation were offered as teaching to the wider community.

Later in seminary, I began serving a large high-profile church—first as a ministry intern and eventually as part of the pastoral staff. This congregation was filled with corporate executives from high-technology industries. Here, the dominant symbol of leadership was the CEO in a corporate boardroom. The great pastoral leaders were those who cast a strong vision, motivated others to creatively implement this vision, and took charge with confidence when necessary. The need for a hierarchy of vision was understood: Effective organizations knew who was in charge. In such an arrangement, being part of the pastoral staff was like being a cabinet member. Just as the fate of each advisor is tied to the fate of the president, our fates were tied to the senior pastor. In this environment, to embarrass or challenge the vision of the senior pastor was a cardinal sin. Our role was to be highly skilled contributors and implementers.

As my own pastoral experience grew larger, a third symbol loomed large—the therapist's couch. As a youth pastor, I regularly encountered students facing adolescent identity issues, the telltale signs of family alcoholism, the residues of family dysfunction, questions of sexual identity, and difficult moral dilemmas. One afternoon, I fielded a call from a young teen from an abusive home who wanted to get an abortion because her pregnancy might prevent her from participating on an international mission team. That same afternoon, a group of parents came to my office expressing concern that the shower their daughters were planning for this same girl sent the wrong message about sexual activity. On days like that, preparing to teach and developing ministry programs seemed like distant memories.

The coming of the emerging culture raises the bar of pastoral expectations even higher. At a recent emergent conference, Kara Powell quipped that contemporary pastors are expected to have "the entrepreneurial skills of Bill Gates, the counseling skills of Dr. Phil, the organizational abilities of Stephen Covey, the authenticity of Oprah, the compassion of Mother Teresa, the courage of William Wallace, and the humor of Jon Stewart."[66] Is it any wonder most pastors feel tremendous professional pressure? How do we make sense of these accelerating expectations?

THE PRESSURES OF THE EMERGING CULTURE AND "LIMINALITY"

Besides the personal frustration of pastoral leaders caught in new expectations, the changes of the emerging culture breed an institutional angst. Alan Roxburgh, a pastor and consultant, teaches that the transition from the modern world to an emerging postmodern world has left us in an era of liminality, a time caught in the gap between modern and postmodern.[67] In this transitional time, leaders still experience the expectations of the waning modernity as well as the expectations of the growing emerging culture.

Jimmy Long, a regional director and leader of the emerging culture initiative within InterVarsity Christian Fellowship, offers some helpful generalizations about this transitional time. He explains that the modern world favored individualism, the courage to make solitary decisions, and an image of invulnerability in its leaders. Leaders were measured by outcomes and given respect because of

---

[66] Kara Eckman Powell, February 3, 2005, in a presentation on Humanity in the learning communities of the Emergent Convention.

[67] Alan Roxburgh, "Pastoral Role in the Missionary Congregation," in *The Church Between Gospel and Culture*, edited by George Hunsberger and Craig Van Gelder (Grand Rapids, Mich.: Wm. B. Eerdmans, 1996), 324-325.

their position in an organization. The emerging, postmodern culture encourages the affirmation and utilization of community, consensual decision-making processes, and a much greater transparency in its leaders. Leaders are measured as much by process as by outcomes, and respect flows from relationship rather than position.[68]

The marked contrasts between modern and postmodern expectations for leadership create an atmosphere ideal for frustration and conflict. No leader likes to feel like an anachronism in a changed culture. This fear strikes at the core for many church leaders. For pastors who were nurtured to take charge as leaders with confidence and contagious vision, a pronouncement of being antiquated or misunderstood comes as a terminal prognosis.

I experienced this conflict in a very personal way when I had to consider a job opportunity that would involve a move to a new community. In decision-making, our family places huge emphasis on vulnerable communication, community participation and blessing, and consensus whenever possible. Following this model, my wife and I formed a discernment group that covenanted to walk with us as we considered our decision. In our early meetings, I was strongly leaning toward moving and taking the new position, but these friends could only offer tepid blessing on that path. They guided us through a process that eventually led to a change in my own perspective about my future direction.

Our decision to stay where we were came as a huge surprise to many people outside our inner circle and was met by a deafening silence from some of my colleagues and other church leaders. Later, as I probed for the source of their silence, I found that some believed I lacked the courage to follow my own obvious preference and had instead passively deferred responsibility to others. I believed the decision to stay in Chapel Hill required a huge amount of courage—this path was fraught with ambiguities and risks. But I was being critiqued for a lack of courage and decisiveness. I may have been a fool, but I didn't feel a like a coward. More significantly, I didn't perceive that either my values or my process of discern-

---

[68] Jimmy is a mentor, friend, and long-standing elder at the Chapel Hill Bible Church. I am deeply indebted to his insights on leadership and modeling of leadership transition.

ment was understood within portions of our church's leadership community.

These radically differing perspectives on my decision-making process are the direct result of the collision of two paradigms for leadership. In seeking community involvement and blessing as I made this critical decision, I was demonstrating what some view as strong and effective leadership. Yet others view those same characteristics as signs of weakness and a lack of courage.

NEW IMAGES: MISSIONAL CHURCH AND PASTOR AS APOSTLE, POET, AND PROPHET

George Hunsberger, Alan Roxburgh, and others in the Gospel in Our Culture Network have done us a great service in exploring new possibilities for envisioning church and pastoral leadership in this time of liminality. Hunsberger describes the church of the recent modern era as a "vendor of religious goods and services" catering to the needs of constituents.[69] With this understanding, it's no wonder pastors in recent modernity have felt such pressure to be skilled in so many different roles: organizers, entrepreneurs, therapists, and spiritual directors.

Today, in a postmodern culture that no longer assumes a Christian consensus or hegemony of values and beliefs, Hunsberger calls the church to become "a body of people sent on a mission."[70] He has coined the phrase "missional church," contending that the church's essential task is to journey with the gospel into a surrounding culture that sees faith as the domain of individuals and questions the value of religious institutions.

Roxburgh takes the next step by suggesting the roles of "apostle," "poet," and "prophet" as metaphors for pastoral leadership in the missional church. He describes the "apostle" as one who leads a congregation to be "witnesses to the gospel in lands where old maps no longer work."[71] The apostle leads the church out of its insular ex-

[69] George Hunsberger, "Sizing up the Shape of the Church," in *The Church Between Gospel and Culture*, edited by George Hunsberger and Craig Van Gelder (Grand Rapids, Mich.: Wm. B. Eerdmans, 1996), 338.
[70] Hunsberger, 341.

perience as a safe harbor from the surrounding culture and into the uncharted seas of postmodernity and the emerging culture.

The pastor as a "poet" hears and expresses the experiences of a congregation. "The poet is a listener and observer, sensing the experience of the body and giving that experience a voice."[72] The poet poignantly narrates the yearnings of a gospel community that seeks to move beyond the dominion of modernity that isolates the story of the gospel from the daily experiences of living.

The pastor as "prophet" leads with the insight and savvy of the Hebrew prophets, who spoke to the impact of cultural realities on the chosen people and their participation in God's redemptive plan. Roxburgh defines the prophet's task as "addressing of the word of God directly into the specific, concrete historical experience of the people of God."[73] The contemporary prophet translates God's revelation into our current cultural realities.

Roxburgh's three images describe viable paths of leadership transition into emerging culture ministry. To minister in the emerging culture, pastoral leadership must guide us into a new context, articulate the narrative of our experiences in this transition, and interpret God's Word into the realities of this new context.

THE PATH OF PLURALITY

The church also needs new structures of leadership to minister effectively in the emerging culture. Many existing churches are transitioning toward greater plurality and community participation in leadership. The communal and experiential attributes of the emerging culture call for leadership structures that are more inclusive and participatory.

I believe one key reason our fellowship at the Chapel Hill Bible Church has thrived through this time of cultural transition is our long history of plurality in leadership. Anticipating many of the

---

[71] Roxburgh, 326.

[72] Roxburgh, 329-330.

[73] Roxburgh, 331.

very issues of postmodernity and highly influenced by the leadership style of university departments, the community of people who founded our fellowship in the 1970s avoided a staffing structure with a senior pastor as the dominant visionary and authority figure. When I arrived in 1990, I was delighted to discover that the pastors were a team of peers, and each one also served as a full member of an elder board that made decisions by consensus. The model was reinforced by a more egalitarian compensation structure, in which the salaries of the pastors were differentiated only because of ministerial experience, not title or position.

Such a structure has allowed us to be more adaptable to cultural change. Since I was immediately given a leadership role and full voice in decision-making, my prophetic perspective on new cultural contexts and realities has been consistently heard and considered. I've not had to "convert" a primary leader to sensitivity about the emerging culture; our leadership design has allowed me and other leaders who bring an understanding of our current culture to have a voice at the table. This has helped us avoid the many unhelpful and oversimplified theological pitfalls that I've described earlier.

In addition to creating space for prophetic and divergent voices, our pluralistic leadership structure has brought other culturally significant consequences. Those in the emergent culture tend to be wary of pastoral leadership that is overly individualized (all roads lead to a single vision), overly professionalized (the province of the ordained), overly technical (a specialized task and function orientation), and spiritually inaccessible (the spiritual life of a pastor being unique from any other person). The emerging culture wants leaders who are vulnerable with their experiences and involved in the life of the community.

The plurality of our professional leadership community has left room and given great voice to lay leadership. Our consensus-model elder board brings lay leaders into direct dialogue and equal authority with the pastors, thereby empowering lay leaders throughout our fellowship. In fact, lay leadership is so assumed that we pastors sometimes have to barge in if we're to have any role at all in some church programs and initiatives!

One wonderful and winsome result of this atmosphere is that it allows our professional leaders to exist as full members of the community. I've asked many other pastors with children if they're ever able to function in the life of their fellowships simply as a parent, rather than always as a pastor. Most said they rarely could "remove the clerical collar" in the community life of their churches. In sharp contrast, I've felt remarkably free to function simply as a "dad" during church events that focus on children. The members of our family participate as full and equal members of the congregation, just as other families do.[74] This atmosphere goes far in shaping the kind of vulnerable and accessible leaders that are demanded by the emerging culture.

EGALITARIAN LEADERSHIP IS NOT A "MAGIC BULLET"

The development of leadership structures that accentuate plurality, participation, and the integration of leaders into community life is essential if churches are to minister effectively in the emerging culture. But moving toward a more egalitarian leadership system is no cure-all. In fact, such a structure brings with it new challenges.

Recalling Roxburgh's view of postmodern leaders as filling the roles of poet, prophet, and apostle, our congregation has found that its egalitarian structure creates safe and ample space for prophetic leadership. Our leaders have been able to speak freely of the implications that the changing cultural context has on our conceptions of Scripture and theology. Poetic leadership has also been affected favorably. Our structure encourages a mosaic of voices describing our community's experience, which is greatly preferable to the singular perspective of a dominating leader.

But this same egalitarian structure has often been an impediment to apostolic leadership. When opportunities arise to move into new territory, our apostles often feel worn down by too much

[74] This attitude is so predominant that on rare occasions—in casual conversation or in formal meetings—I have to interject that, as a professional pastor, my perspective on or experience of a particular event or decision is a bit different!

discussion and analysis. The painstaking process of seeking the full community's permission and approval can greatly diminish the passion of a vision and may result in missed opportunities. Our community has struggled with this issue throughout its lifespan.

Ironically, we've also seen cases where these very same dynamics have caused apostolic leadership within the congregation to flourish. Lay leaders who are savvy enough to develop visions and initiatives while avoiding formal approval have produced marvelous ministries, furthering our atmosphere of community leadership. Yet at other times, efforts to avoid the communal decision-making process have led to redundant initiatives that sap resources and accentuate divisions. This can put formal leadership in the awkward position of having to slow down initiatives or choose between conflicting options, rather than enthusiastically blessing our community's ministry.

An egalitarian leadership environment like ours also requires significant time commitments in team communication. Pastoral leadership for our fellowship has been shared by as many as five co-pastors with radically differing personalities and gifts.[75] To function effectively, we committed to meet regularly and to have regular retreats together. We came up with a unique set of rules for our annual retreats. Each pastor would take roughly an hour to describe—without interruption—the state of our team and our church and to ask for the team's counsel on any personal or professional matter. Then the team would speak to this person "for as long as was deemed necessary!" Each year, it seemed like a different person would need well over a day's worth of feedback, challenge, or discernment. These annual pilgrimages produced amazing moments of self-discovery and a profound sense of understanding and community among the members of an intentionally diverse team.[76]

---

[75] This was truly a team of unique gifts and marvelous skills. One pastor led the teaching that defined our ethos and energized decades of effective ministry. Another pastor accepted the mantle of internal and civic hospitality and became the "face" of our leadership team—both inside the body and to our local community. Still another pastor spent his primary energies in blessing ministries, overseeing the organization of our team, and communicating with other leadership teams in the body. My role included the prophetic functions of analyzing our team community and our surrounding culture (a quasi systems counselor and sociologist).

[76] Without a doubt, our university-based community provided great impetus for this model. The typical academic department (one that is chaired by an individual who is a peer to many fully tenured faculty members) influenced our structure and provided many leaders who could function well under these expectations. Others in our community—particularly corporate leaders and entrepreneurs—have sometimes struggled to operate in this environment.

The costs in time, dialogue, and vulnerability were high, but many of the results were marvelous. Our congregational community reflected the great diversity of our pastoral team in politics, lifestyles, theology (within a general consensus), and socioeconomics. Without a singular leader whose individual vision provided the church's direction, our congregation was free to express a variety of diverse missions. The commitment to formal and informal lay leadership was astounding. Laypersons throughout our fellowship were filling roles that might be full-time staff positions in many congregations of comparable size. Our lay elders exhibited an astounding commitment to ministry and radical lifestyles that reflected the teachings of Jesus.

There were many challenges in adopting an egalitarian leadership structure; but from my perspective, these kinds of challenges are preferable to those resulting from an authoritative and impersonal leadership's attempts to motivate a community to action. We continue to struggle to empower apostolic leadership without creating a centralized structure that destroys our ethos. It's a work in progress that strongly cautions against adamant conclusions.

Part of the answer for us involved desacralizing the idol of egalitarian leadership. We still believe the radical ideal of community leadership should be preserved and protected. But we've learned over the past 15 years that creating some hierarchy and lines of authority/responsibility are not necessarily refutations of this ideal. Tim Keel, founding pastor of Jacob's Well in Kansas City, told me he felt he said "we" far too often in describing the direction of the church in its earliest days—long before they were truly a "we." He now believes it would have been more accurate at that stage to say "I" in reference to the direction in which he was leading the fellowship in its earliest years. I've spent time with the staff of Jacob's Well on several occasions, and the level of community and ministry ownership there is quite evident. Keel's observation affirms that strong apostolic leadership is often necessary and doesn't preclude shared leadership.

Deep into our own journey, our staff and congregation have realized the egalitarian structure is not the true value, nor should the structure remain invulnerable to critique. The real value has been the formation of a shared, diverse community leadership environment that is not oriented around the gifts, vision, and idiosyncrasies of a single individual.

LISTENING TO SOUL AND CULTURE

I've recently been in discussion with faculty at the Mars Hill Graduate School in Seattle as the school seeks to redesign its Master of Divinity program. Their queries of seminary graduates and prospective students confirmed what many have long known: Traditional theological education has left many aspects of ministry leadership underdeveloped or even unaddressed. Seminaries tend to focus on preparing pastors to study the Bible and theology, and to preach with skill and passion. Most schools have added therapeutic skills and program management to the training curriculum. But some of the qualities most essential for effective ministry in the emerging culture are often absent or marginalized in our leadership preparations.

Ministry today demands sensitivity to both soul and culture. In an era where vulnerability and authenticity are highly prized among leaders, pastors must learn to hear the voice of God in the narrative of broken and turbulent lives—and confront their own brokenness. They also must learn to sense the movement of God in our culture, as well as the cry of shame and anguish in our communities. In response to these needs, Mars Hill has crafted their ministry training around the three foci of soul, text, and culture. This is an appropriate lead to follow, as we prepare leaders for ministry in the emerging culture.

In my life of ministry I've experienced a great transition that many friends and colleagues also describe. In my first five years after seminary, I ran on enthusiasm, energy, and giftedness. But as I transitioned into my 30s, my theology collided with experiences that challenged previous certainties. Working empathetically with teens who were accumulating a range of hurts and life experiences, my own wounds and failures became increasingly difficult to ignore. This recognition brought me to a point of crisis—I could either explore my own narrative and pain in order to better integrate these into my life and ministry, or I could change my direction—perhaps leaving ministry as a vocation.

In my case, the primary issue was that I'd never really grieved nor integrated into my personal theology the tragic death of a parent during my teens. Thankfully, I stumbled into a series of wonderful experiences of soul care and spiritual direction that encouraged me through a process of grieving. Then I integrated these wounds into my soul conversation with God and my theological reflection of God's presence in our world. But like many other young pastors, I was completely unprepared for this prayerful and reflective work.

I've known too many women and men in pastoral leadership positions whose theology and ministry practices are precariously detached from their personal stories and observations about our culture. I've known male pastors who counsel or supervise women, yet they've never addressed their insecurities with the primary feminine figures in their personal stories. Other church leaders seem completely unaware of how the dynamics of their family of origin have made an indelible imprint on their communications and personal interactions. I've known leaders who allow their great enthusiasm in ministry to mask a profound disappointment with God in their personal story. The examples are endless. For some, the changes in culture I've described throughout the book create feelings of fear, inadequacy, or confusion that lead to personal crises.

In our previous discussion of the Bible, we saw that, when it's read in conjunction with the experiences of the human soul and the narratives of our many cultures, Scripture becomes a living "text," expressing the powerful reality of God's redemptive work instead of a static compendium of theological truths. Our ability to hear God through Scripture suffers from our lack of fluency in the experiences of the soul and a deafened ear directed at the story of culture. Sadly, in the liminality of great cultural changes that require leaders who can be transparent, vulnerable, and skilled in the languages of culture and community, many leaders find themselves marginally equipped to enter this new world.

I hearken back to Tim Keel's comment that it might have been more accurate if he'd used the pronoun "I" instead of "we" in forging the early direction of the Jacob's Well community. When I imagine Tim using these words, knowing that his leadership and teaching of Scripture has been deeply shaped by the exegesis of soul and culture, his use of "I" is a gentle and bold invitation for a community to embrace an apostolic direction, rather than a demand to be followed.

NEW ECONOMICS OF LEADERSHIP

The realities of the emerging culture not only require new skills for leaders, but they are also shaping new economic models for church leadership.

Nairobi Chapel in Kenya is one of the most bold and visionary churches in the world. Their modest-sized stone building is nestled among the dormitories of the University of Nairobi, near the city's downtown business district. Senior Pastor Oscar Muiru leads multiple congregations filled with students, internationals, and corporate leaders. He also leads a marvelously gifted, large, and diverse staff team of women and men.

Over the last two decades, Kenya has faced a continual decline in economics and urban infrastructure. Pastor Muiru has led the congregations of Nairobi Chapel to realize that they could push forward with their vision (which calls for dividing into five regional fellowships and planting 200 new churches) only if they were to develop a new economic model. Today, Muiru and the four other members of the senior pastoral staff are all working as entrepreneurs seeking to develop self-sustaining businesses. Their goal is to have income from these businesses replace a sizable portion of their salaries in the near future. Even though members of the congregation expect to have fewer resources with each passing year, the pastors' desire is to see the church's resources go to expanding the staff and outreach of the congregation.

Recent U.S. economics remind us that our congregations cannot count on unbridled financial growth in perpetuity. The fluctuations of our economy notwithstanding, our culture's movement toward a more post-Christian era may have an even greater impact on the economics of ministry. Currently, much local church growth is the simple result of population growth among persons seeking to attend church. As we look toward a more post-Christian society, we can easily envision declining church attendance and resources. Additionally, the relational nature of the emerging culture has motivated the formation of smaller missional communities that will certainly have fewer resources than the larger churches that now fill our cultural landscape.

These changing conditions portend an entirely different resource environment for the church and its leaders in the future. Almost daily, I hear friends in emerging culture ministry say things like, "I've got to find an appropriate job or profession so I can continue to do ministry." We are moving to a time when more ministry leaders will be bivocational with their primary incomes coming from alternative sources. In our church, Jim Thomas serves as a bivocational pastor, leading our cross-cultural mission initiatives while also serving as a professor of epidemiology in the University of North Carolina's School of Public Health. Jim has had to work creatively and flexibly to manage the tension between his two professions, but the arrangement has been a blessing beyond measure for our fellowship. Jim's professional interest and expertise in sexually transmitted diseases, including AIDS, has invigorated church programs and ministries related to the AIDS pandemic. Jim is truly an apostle who is leading us into new horizons of ministry with amazing results.

Many ministries are developing businesses and entrepreneurial endeavors not only as income streams, but also as vital bridges into the emerging culture. While it was once considered dangerous and taboo in the very compartmentalized church of modernity, the church-business enterprises have great potential for providing a hospitable foyer for those in our surrounding culture to enter our fellowships and communities. One need only look to the local coffeehouse to acknowledge this reality. Filled with sofas, comfortable chairs, large tables, outlets for laptop users, and beautiful local artwork, the coffeehouse has become the public living room for our culture. Churches and missional communities are already hosting cafés, recording studios, Web-design businesses, art galleries, and studios for artists.

Such developments will have a major impact on theological education and ministry preparation. Leaders will increasingly be trained to lead and serve in missional communities and be proficient in other professions. New emphasis will be placed on a creative integration of multiple work environments and communities. Ministry structures will need to be adjusted to allow for the participation of bivocational leaders.

Changes in the vision and images of pastoral ministry, the skill sets required, and even the economics of ministry leadership point toward a corresponding need for change in how we think of and nurture community. In the next chapter, we'll look at those changing expectations for community formation.

Transition in Community Formation

I once served as a consultant for a church that was involved in a fairly typical struggle over worship style. Several members of the congregation wanted their worship to incorporate more contemporary music, but the pastor was resistant for a variety of reasons. In one conversation the pastor told these members that he'd begin using specific songs from contemporary genres once they'd passed the test of time and had been proven fruitful for the worship life of the church. In response, one person noted the obvious: by then, the music would no longer be contemporary. In this conflict, the pastor was employing a standard that was highly determinative of the outcome.

Of course, our interests, values, and prejudices will influence any decision we face. This is not only true of individuals, but also of organizations—including the church. I believe many modern and existing churches have a number of prejudices about community formation that deeply impair or even preclude their ability to transition into effective emerging culture ministry. But before we look at how we might overcome some of these prejudices, it's helpful to consider the historic relationship between church and culture that has shaped their development.

CONSTANTINE AND "OFFICIAL" RELIGION

In the first few centuries after Jesus' time on earth, Christianity was an odd, marginalized, and threatened way of life in the Roman Empire. To be Christian was inherently countercultural. The apostle Peter's labeling of the fledgling Christian community as "aliens and strangers" to their culture made perfect sense (1 Peter 2:11).

The conversion of the Roman emperor Constantine in 313 AD—and the subsequent installment of Christianity as the official religion of the West—changed the cultural trajectory of Christianity dramatically. The church went from being textbook "outsiders" to ultimate "insiders." From that point on, the church would take its organizational and doctrinal shape from a position of favor and status within Western society. Peter's description of Christians as "aliens and strangers" would increasingly seem like a quaint anachronism.

In *A Peculiar People*, author Rodney Clapp writes about this rags-to-riches cultural shift commonly called "Constantinianism." Clapp explains that in this shift, the church moved from the dominant question of *How can we survive and remain faithful Christians under Caesar?* to a new question: *How can we adjust the church's expectations so Caesar can consider himself a faithful Christian?*[77] While forces such as the Reformation, the Enlightenment, industrialization, and rapid advances in technology have surely made their mark on modern Christianity, Clapp believes the church still continues to struggle profoundly with the Constantinian question: *How can we create a community identity distinct from our surrounding culture, yet retain our favored status?*

The values, attributes, and contours of Western culture have shaped, both subtly and overtly, the church's defaults and prejudices regarding community formation. But the coming of postmodernity has brought on what Clapp describes as a time of delicious irony. At a moment when Western civilization has reached a zenith of economic, cultural, military, and technological dominance, it's declared that it no longer needs the church as its sole, religious sponsor.[78] Standing on the threshold of postmodernity, Western culture looks with embarrassment at its past alliance with Christianity.

For Clapp and theologians like Stanley Hauerwas, there could hardly be better news. Divested from its alignment with the Western establishment and restored to its original status as "strangers and aliens," the church is free to be the church again.[79] Caesar will be challenged once again to embrace an authentic Christianity. As we cross the threshold into postmodernity, the church has a unique opportunity to confront the prejudices and predispositions of community formation that took root during modernity and the long Constantinian dominance of the church in culture. During this transition, many of our defaults regarding community formation will require reconsideration and reformation.

---

[77] Rodney Clapp, *A Peculiar People* (Downers Grove, Ill.: InterVarsity Press, 1996), 26.

[78] Clapp, 17.

[79] See also Stanley Hauerwas and William H. Willimon, *Resident Aliens* (Nashville: Abingdon Press, 1989).

DEFAULT: DOCTRINE AS GUARDIAN OF THE GATE

When I was in seminary, another student invited me to have lunch with a new professor whose academic pedigree included a staunch, reformed theological heritage. During this meeting, I played the role of devil's advocate, asking a wide range of theological questions. Sensing this professor's growing discomfort, my friend blurted out, "It's okay. Tim believes in a limited atonement." The lunch instantly relaxed. I was okay. I had been identified as existing within doctrinally defined boundaries of community. My questions were reclassified as the wonderings of a curious mind, not the challenges of someone outside the fold. While it is rarely this blatant, doctrine and belief often play a dominant role in defining who is and who isn't part of our church communities.

In many churches, the process of becoming a member or joining a leadership team is reduced to doctrinal tests. Sadly, I've seen more than my fair share of new member interviews where prospective members showed up anxiously expecting a theological exam—despite many public disclaimers to the contrary. In conservative church settings, there is often great reluctance to receive new members who don't profess an evangelical description of their faith, even if their lives manifest ample evidence of the presence of God's Spirit. At our new member interviews, I've sometimes wondered aloud whether or not Mother Teresa could successfully join our fellowship. We've concluded that she probably could become a member—but some folks would surely be nervous about the decision! The right doctrine and language have become the centerpieces of community formation.

Don't misunderstand me: I strongly affirm the importance of doctrine in the life of the church. My own spiritual life is probably overly formed in theological reading and Scripture analysis. But I believe that allowing doctrine to dominate the process of joining Christian community is theologically, functionally, and missionally challenged.

Theological Challenges

There is no theological consensus about entry into the Christian community, although the role of faith is usually considered central. Some Christian traditions emphasize the baptism of children as a rite of initiation that invokes a covenant relationship with the church and anticipates personal faith. Others emphasize identification with Jesus' life and teachings through personal faith as the first port of entry. The New Testament records many distinct narratives of entry. The thief crucified beside Jesus (Luke 23:43) is welcomed on the basis of a simple and prayerful plea to Jesus. Mark records a remarkable scene where a small band of men lower a paralyzed friend through the roof to the very feet of Jesus, who seems to forgive the sins of the paralytic based on the faith of those who brought him there (Mark 2:5)! Nicodemus' journey toward faith (John 3:1-21) includes the kind of theological dialogue and inquiry that might parallel an Alpha course or investigative Bible study in the contemporary church.

We often use the term *conversion* to describe a person's entry into Christian community. In his study of this term, Dick Peace has contrasted the entry experiences of Jesus' disciples with Paul's experience.[80] Peace notes that Paul's Damascus Road encounter with the risen Christ (Acts 9) is considered the primary model of Christian conversion. However, although Paul's conversion seemingly happens in a single moment, it still involves three spiritual movements: insight, turning, and transformation.[81]

Peace then turns to the book of Mark, noting the gospel writer's interest in journaling the long conversion process of Jesus' closest community—the disciples. These followers of Jesus experience an arduous and sometimes frustrating journey to faith. They are front-row witnesses to numerous healings, exorcisms, and powerful teachings before they gain the insight that Jesus is indeed the promised Messiah. They are even sent out in pairs to preach the good news before they fully understand Jesus' identity (Mark 6:7-13)! They struggle to understand the meaning of Jesus' death, and

[80] Richard V. Peace, *Conversion in the New Testament* (Grand Rapids, Mich.: Wm. B. Eerdmans, 1999).
[81] Peace, 25-26.

they must confront their own jealousies regarding the rewards of the kingdom Jesus promises. Only at the other end of this journey—*after* Jesus' resurrection—is it really accurate to call them disciples.

Peace reminds us that there are many paths into Christian community. Paul's conversion involves a single profound event that challenges him to rethink his life and theological perspective. The conversions of the disciples parallel the typical "postmodern conversion," where a person first enters into a community and it's the involvement with that community that ultimately transforms the whole of his or her life. Doctrine can and does play a significant role in both cases. But it's theologically inaccurate to reduce conversion to doctrinal affirmation or the transfer of theological information.

Functional Challenges

It can be tempting to rely on doctrine to shape the boundaries of community. It feels reassuring to have an easy measure of who is "in" and who is "out." But our craving for this certainty, in determining the boundaries of community, can blind us to the functional weakness of this approach. The doctrinal approach to community formation doesn't work consistently. And when it fails, there can be huge casualties in community life.

Recently, a young couple arrived on my doorstep in tears. Before getting engaged, they had sought their parents' blessings, only to discover the potential groom's parents had huge reservations. His girlfriend didn't seem "Christian enough" for them. From my perspective, this young woman had experienced a remarkable journey of commitment and fellowship with Christ over the past year. And her story inspired many in our community. What she lacked was a doctrinal and theological background—which could come only from many years of study and Christian teaching. This young couple had a strong and developing understanding of the place of marriage in worship, mission, and community. In my opinion, the snap judgment of the groom's family was obscuring their ability to see that their son had chosen a wonderful partner.

There is great diversity in Christian doctrine; and the language of any stream of Christian thought can seem exclusive, inaccessible, or misleading to others. I once received a blistering critique of a series of talks I had given. My young critic, a graduate student, charged that I had ignored the truth of the gospel when I encouraged the audience to "define their lives by Jesus' story" and "to seek the face of God." After each of these critiques, he added, "Whatever that means!" Obviously, I have a vested interest in the situation, but I don't believe we have a case of heresy or pastoral malpractice here. Instead, first and foremost we have a language problem. I didn't use the theological language favored by this student; therefore, my points were frivolous, obtuse, or even scandalous. I hope this student's critique will lead us into a fruitful conversation. (I certainly have things to learn from his concerns.) But the situation points to how a heavy-handed use of specific doctrines or language can produce needless hurt and great breaches in community.

Missional Challenges

A doctrinal approach to community formation also has significant missional liabilities. One common axiom of emerging culture ministry is the declaration that emerging culture persons will join a community before affirming the beliefs of that community. In other words, emerging culture persons place *belonging* before *believing*. Using doctrine as the doorkeeper essentially slams shut the front door of the church in the face of spiritual seekers. These persons need to enter and participate in community as part of their search for spiritual truth and goodness. In fact, they are far more likely to make their spiritual discernment based on the quality and characteristics of a community, rather than its doctrinal propositions.[82]

In reality, using doctrine as a doorway may lead more easily to the illusion of theological homogeneity rather than the reality of it. Within most congregations there is a wide spectrum of theological diversity.[83] As one who has the privilege of hearing people's honest theological questions, the range of doctrinal assumptions in our fellowship constantly amazes me. Query persons in our church about

---

[82] This does not mean that belief systems and doctrinal propositions are unnecessary or antiquated in any way. Instead, it implies that theological inquiry and doctrinal study will occur in later stages of community formation. They will also take different forms.

[83] This is also true of confessional congregations that adhere to a specific confession or creed.

what they really believe about hell, the sacraments, and a variety of challenging biblical texts, and you'll be amazed at the variety of responses!

This gap between the perception of homogeneity and the reality of theological diversity can have unfortunate missional consequences. Emerging culture persons are looking for honest, authentic community dialogue in response to spiritual questions. The dependence on doctrinal agreement as the gateway to community and the inevitable realizations of theological diversity within Christian communities create "don't ask, don't tell" environments that are the antithesis of the honest dialogue sought by postmodern people. We too often propagate an inaccurate (and, in some cases, dishonest) declaration of theological homogeneity and then send the message that those who question it or think differently are not tolerated. These are seeds of missional disaster as the emerging culture gains strength.[84]

We live in an era of great diversity of thought in culture and significant doctrinal diversity within the church. A doctrinally dominated approach to community formation threatens to accentuate dishonesty within our communities and division among Christian communities. At a time when division among Christ-followers is a great barrier to the gracious redemption Jesus offers to the world, authenticity in dialogue is an essential rule of ministry.

A COMMITMENT TO INCLUSION

Our churches don't need to replace doctrine with a more effective guard at the door of community participation. We need to strongly question the importance of placing any barriers at the church's doors. With many people seeking access to church communities before engaging their doctrinal distinctives and belief narratives, we must begin to develop community formation models based on inclusion.

---

[84] This is the youth ministry dilemma many pastors face. Their teens have grown up under emerging culture assumptions of dialogue and mystery. They have also been born inside the church rather than having to enter from the outside. An authentic and effective youth ministry must give them room to ask questions and challenge the assumptions of the community. Spiritual formation stage theorists affirm this questioning and challenging as part of spiritual growth. This freedom to question often collides with a church perception that such questioning is unnecessary (since we all entered through the same door) and inappropriate. Many an effective youth pastor or youth ministry shrivels in this environment!

This is going to be extremely difficult for fellowships that profess exclusivist views on salvation and eternity. For these churches (our church is one), the example of Jesus is paramount. Jesus often used exclusivist language in talking about salvation and judgment (wheat/tares, sheep/goats). Despite this language, Jesus made continual, open invitations to join him in community. We need to replicate the content and spirit of these invitations to minister effectively in the emerging culture.

When I served as a youth pastor, the youth in our ministry were almost evenly split between those who professed a Christian commitment and those who did not. This provided a wonderfully honest atmosphere to pursue and challenge the Christian faith. I was somewhat surprised to find that the students who didn't profess faith were just as likely to attend events that involved a high level of spiritual inquiry or participation. In fact, they were far less likely to attend entertainment-based programs than those students who'd made a Christian commitment.

Many kids who wouldn't have called themselves Christians were also eager participants and gifted contributors on a variety of short-term, cross-cultural mission teams over the years. Not only did they grow spiritually, but also their presence helped create a spiritually nourishing environment for our team and hosts. But we had to make several adjustments in community formation to facilitate this situation. For example, the first question on our team applications had been, "Why are you a Christian and how do you know it?" (Note the doctrinal entry point!) We changed the application and our attitude about team participation. We were also diligent and honest with prospective hosts about our teams. We made a commitment that we'd accept no projects that would exclude any student. Each team crafted a covenant that was sensitive to the diversity of the team, yet unambiguous in its commitment to the values of Christian mission and community.

Our emphasis on inclusiveness and diversity helped transform these teams into dynamic communities that pursued the Christian path with a vibrant commitment to relationship, honesty, and dialogue. Our mission projects helped the kids who already had a Christian commitment grow in their faith and understanding of the world. But they were not "Christian pep-rally" experiences that resulted in a "retreat high"; nor were they watered-down spiritual communities with a common interest in serving a distant culture.

Our youth enthusiastically explored and experienced spiritual practices such as praying the hours, the Ignatian examen, and *lectio divina.* They also diligently studied some of the most culturally challenging Scripture texts. These open-ended communities ministered to my own wounds and gave me hope (when hope was hard to find) about the power of God's presence in our world. After many years of these experiences, I began to realize we weren't just running mission teams; we were developing a model of missional community that has become the basis for our current trajectories in community formation and ministry.[85]

DEFAULT: SACRED INDIVIDUALISM

I've already discussed how the deep-seated individualism of our culture encourages us to eschew the diversities of real community for more homogenous gatherings that affirm our personal lifestyles and interests.[86] What are some other effects of individualism on community formation?

The growing secularism of modernity fashions religious faith as purely an individual, private matter. The Christian church, in its privileged position as state religion in the West, has been dismayed to observe its empires and emperors becoming demonstratively less interested in Christianity. As a result, the church has allowed and even promoted the sentiment that religion is the province of private personal piety. In this move toward the interiorization of faith, the church's primary demand of the state has been to protect individual, religious liberties.

---

[85] In chapters 9 and 11, I will expound on this essential path of missional community.

[86] This is one premise that Robert Bellah makes persuasively in *Habits of the Heart* (Berkeley, Calif.: Univ. of California Press, 1985), 72-75. See chapter 2 for more discussion on this tendency.

Recently, I was listening to a sports-talk radio discussion critiquing athletes who thank God profusely and publicly for their performances. I agree that these acts of praise can be shallow and obnoxious. But the host took it a step further by adamantly asserting that religion is solely a personal and private matter. In his view, public affirmations of faith were offensive and intrusive, and they defied the substance of what it meant to be religious. This is the privatization of late Constantinianism in a media sound bite. And it's totally contrary to the gospel of Jesus, which demands a courageous public faith—a faith that seeks to usher in a kingdom that would overturn the injustices of society and shake the world to its core.

The religious privatization and rising individualism of Western society have had devastating effects on community formation in the church. It should be said emphatically that churches can demonstrate a remarkable upgrade from community experiences in our culture. But in far too many cases, we act as if the primary function of Christian community is to protect individual rights and interests. In this manner, we give the church the same vacuous job description as the state—protecting our personal rights and liberties.

Two stories help illustrate this phenomenon. In a congregational meeting, our church was facing some discomfort and angst about our budget. Although a tight budget was the lightning rod of the conversation, the real concerns pertained to the direction of the ministry being financed. A long-time attendee shared his great displeasure with the proposed budget and wondered why the leadership had not offered a fiscal alternative for those who didn't want to participate in this community commitment. The implication was that the community must not only protect the individual interests and desires of each member, but also proactively provide outlets for these. Though it's rarely expressed this blatantly, amid our highly privatized understandings of faith in a culture saturated with individualism, many see community solely as a champion of this sacred individualism. Submitting our individual preferences to community commitments and covenants can be a foreign notion in our fellowships.

A second story further illustrates sacred individualism, and it also reveals the modern/postmodern fault line running right through many fellowships. When we utilized an entire morning worship service to launch our emerging culture mission initiative, the sermon time was given to a dialogue that was intended to reinforce the mission, to offer opportunity to discuss its challenges, and to invite the community's participation. Some members were highly frustrated by this, feeling that an advertisement for a new activity had replaced a sacred spiritual event—the sermon! I'm biased, of course, but I saw this presentation as an act of spiritual communication by some in our community, inviting wider participation in what we perceive as a movement of God's Spirit in our midst.

For some, a sermon is a learning event or even a challenge that speaks to the interior, personal spiritual life of an individual. From this perspective, community missional opportunity, dialogue, and celebration are all separate from (or perhaps the result of) personal and private spirituality. But for those in our congregation who see their individual faith as holistically integrated with community participation and mission, this "sermon" was affirmed as one of our best ever.

The postmodern world desperately needs to see a community that lives out the Christian story. A church committed to protecting individual rights and liberties will fail utterly in this missional need!

ADDING "COMMUNITY" TO COMMUNITY FORMATION

We must move beyond false understandings of community oriented only toward protecting individual interests or separating believers from the surrounding culture. But how can our fellowships add "community" back into our efforts of community formation? Two paradigm shifts can help facilitate this transformation.

First, we need to change our primary metaphor for community. In many churches, the concept of community is like a golf team—

everyone goes out and shoots his or her individual round and then the personal scores are added together to create a team score. Oh sure, you may share a golf cart, tee box, or green with teammates or competitors, but it's up to each individual member of the team to execute their shots.

Contrast that with a football team, where every player has a unique assignment integral to the success of each play. Players in high profile positions—quarterbacks, running backs, and wide receivers—dominate our attention. But when an anonymous lineman misses a blocking assignment, the whole play is destroyed.

This illustration points toward a critical need for the church to reconceive community in a culture that protects individual freedoms at all costs.[87] We regularly speak of community as a series of personal actions—specific acts of service, words of encouragement, prayer for others, and personal confrontations ("speaking the truth with love"). Indeed, these are all components of community living. But what is sometimes missing is a concept of community that transcends the individual. Too many times the aforementioned activities are considered in terms of personal gifts, personal spiritual needs, and personal boundaries. The language of community is strangely absent. Our conversations about community involvement regularly begin with an individualistic frame of reference. It can be rare in our fellowships for someone to approach a leader and ask to hear the narrative of the community—its needs and its passions—as a starting point for community involvement.

A second paradigm shift involves deconstructing the false dichotomy between inwardly focused and outwardly focused ministries. This split was painfully obvious to me as a youth pastor. Parents regularly asked me if a particular event or program was intended for "discipleship" or "outreach." This question assumes discipleship and spiritual growth are personal and best accomplished without the distractions (or temptations) of a diverse community being present. The corollary assumption is that outreach has nothing to do with spiritual formation. This distinction typically car-

---

[87] As a lover of baseball and soccer who laments the seemingly unending time stoppages of football and admires the unobtainable (for me) skill of playing golf, this metaphor is painful and should be taken only so far!

ries linear, sequential, and compartmentalized implications. One first experiences spiritual growth and then chooses to participate in outreach activities like evangelism or social justice. The inward-outward dichotomy is really an individual-community dichotomy that sees and values individuals as separate from their communities. When asked this question by parents, I was always quick to reply that spiritual formation happens best and most completely in the context of community and mission.

Community expands our understanding of God beyond the limits of our individual experiences and personalities. Acts of mission form us spiritually in addition to being motivated by our spiritual growth. Breaking this dichotomy between inward-focused ministries and those directed outward helps put community back into a sacred place in the church. When the inward-outward firewall is left unchallenged, we not only reinforce a sacred individualism, but also run the risk of allowing consumerism, personal preferences, and individual needs to dominate the discourse within Christian community.

Leadership is essential in encouraging these paradigm shifts. Previously, I emphasized Alan Roxburgh's exposition of emerging leaders as poets, prophets, and apostles. The poetic role is particularly significant in creating a vision and language that begins with community rather than individualism as its orienting perspective. Poet-leaders telling the historical narrative of a faith community— as well as its present wounds, dynamics, and directionality—will challenge our predisposition to idolize individualism and to overly individualize spiritual formation. Prophetic leadership that courageously describes the perils of our cultural surroundings can help reconnect culture and community with spiritual formation. And apostolic leadership can direct individuals and communities out of insulated environments into new experiences of mission and relationship that enhance the role of community and spiritual formation within the church.

BEYOND LIKENESS, FRAGMENTATION, AND COMPETITION

Before concluding our discussion of community formation, let's take a quick look at three other factors that can be monumental barriers to building community if they're left unaddressed. Each of these is a specific expression of the sacred individualism that threatens community formation in the contemporary church.

Likeness

Likeness is sometimes thought of as the answer to creating community within many congregations. Long ago, churches discovered that grouping people by their similarities could be tremendously expedient in terms of numerical and program growth. In some churches, as soon as you make it through the front door, you're directed down channels based on your age, gender, marital status, and interests. This can be valuable in some ways. But there are significant dangers in a preponderance of ministries based on likeness.

Several years ago, when our two children were still quite young, my wife, Mimi, escaped to the grocery store for some quiet shopping. While there, she bumped into another woman from our church who was a good friend, also in her mid-30s, and single without kids. After sharing a warm hug, her friend exclaimed that it was so good to experience an embrace because she felt like she was "the most undertouched woman on earth." Mimi added that, as the mom of a physical three-year-old and a one-year-old, she sometimes felt like the most overtouched woman on earth. These two women had grown up near each other, attended the same university, and had led remarkably similar lives through their college days. But since then, their journeys were significantly different. One entered the corporate world. The other became an artist. One married and had children. The other stayed single. They shared a community life in the same church but had vastly different stories to tell.

Far more divergent stories exist in even the most homogenous of churches. When I preach, I like to look at the faces within our congregation. I often marvel at the diversity there. I see financially struggling graduate students who live in student housing sitting beside peers in the corporate world who've just upsized to a larger home; a homeschooling mom with five school-age children sitting next to a business consultant with two kids in a private school. Red-staters and blue-staters share a smirk about the same joke. Duke fans and Carolina fans worship together, for crying out loud. (This chapter is being written in March!) An advocate for the Defense of Marriage Act might be shocked to learn she was sharing a row with a gay couple that is currently seeking a civil union. Surely there are people whose lives are enmeshed in the postmodern assumptions of the emerging culture worshipping right next to folks who firmly believe the emerging culture conversation is a heretical distraction from truth. What would it be like if we really talked to each other, instead of grouping with those most like us?

I'm not on a crusade against all age-specific or gender-specific ministries. But the predominance of ministry strategies and programs based on likeness works strongly against stories from different journeys being told in our churches. I've found the telling of divergent stories to be one of the most effective paths for churches to develop sensitivity to the issues and realties of the emerging culture.

As I've shared repeatedly, my church's dialogue with the emerging culture and the emerging church has ranged from creative and imaginative to cautious and fearful. Given this reality, I marvel that our fellowship voted (nearly unanimously) to devote significant staff time and funding to a major emerging culture mission initiative. Many who admit they don't fully understand the sensitivities and value of the emerging church movement blessed this effort. Frequently I'm asked how the emerging culture conversation ended up front and center in such a congregation. Part of the answer lies in this arena of community formation.[88]

One historic strength of our fellowship is our ability to resist

[88] The second key answer to this question lies in missional transition, which is the subject of chapter 9.

some forms of segregation and talk to one another across our differences. In fact, I've often seen the interests of divergent perspectives defended by persons who don't share those perspectives. I fondly remember a moment when an excited member of the Christian Coalition dropped by our office to provide voting guides and other informational materials for our foyer. A politically conservative staff member (who had a family member running for state office whose campaign was enthusiastically endorsed in these guides) greeted this guest warmly, but then explained that we didn't want political materials that might convey that a diversity of political opinion was not welcome in our congregation.

I'm always delighted when a member of our church tells me how the diversity within our congregation has stretched them spiritually. I'd never claim that our impulse to affirm diversity is applied evenly to every issue, nor that our dialogue is always positive. But our tendency toward diversity over likeness has allowed emerging culture stories and concerns to be told to many persons who have less access to this perspective. When we find ways to allow our different stories to be told, the emerging culture becomes less of a threat from the outside and more of a ministry opportunity and act of sensitivity to the person who sits right beside me in church.

Fragmentation

A second factor affecting community formation is the persistent fragmentation of our lives. My own household illustrates this. We live in a splendid—and occasionally irritating—intersection between three different cities with different socioeconomics, school systems, calendars, universities, politics, and opportunities. These differences invite fragmentation. Our kids play soccer in one community and baseball in another. Our Christian community is primarily located in Durham, but athletic and alumni activities take us to Chapel Hill. We pay our local taxes to Durham but have a Chapel Hill mailing address. Our lives, like those of so many other Americans, are testimonies of fragmentation based on multiple opportunities and choices.

Many of us in this culture have more relational obligations than we can handle, yet we complain about the lack of depth in these relationships. We interact with a myriad of people, but few people really know us. Sometimes we feel we have too much "community," but no true community. Such fragmentation breeds autonomous decision-making based on consumerism, individualism, and personal preferences. (After all, who really knows us well enough to help?)

Even when it desires to do so, the typical church has great difficulty combating fragmentation. Most large churches don't have the space or capability to bring everyone together at the same time, even if such an event could be constructed. Our churches are then forced to provide more choices and options that further divide our lives. Even churches that are highly committed to intergenerational ministry face the limitations of infrastructure and budget.

A missing value challenge in this dilemma is a call to missional proximity—consolidating our relational, vocational, recreational, political, and purchasing lives in specific communities. We've long neglected to encourage our congregants to be intentional in the neighborhoods they choose. The same intentionality should apply to political activity, recreational involvement, where we spend our money, and how we share the open spaces in our lives with others.

The call to missional proximity is a powerful antidote to idolatrous individualism and the fragmentation that drives our lives to anonymity and exhaustion. In many ways, missional proximity encourages churches toward more of a parish model for ministry, where the congregation's mission is shaped and determined by the needs of the immediate community. It also invites us to break down the idolatrous lines we draw that isolate our families from our communities and culture. Our lives and churches feel profoundly irrelevant to emerging culture persons when we only dabble in the local as consumers and transients, never learning the narratives and needs of our local community.

Competition

Adopting a parish approach that emphasizes localized ministry will shape our response to a final cultural force affecting community formation—competition. In a capitalistic society, the program, product, business, or community that survives is the one that wins. Market forces deem this an ironclad axiom. As a result, we are competitive to the core of our beings. It should be noted that competition is an act of separation and individualism. We separate ourselves from the pack by winning. We distinguish ourselves from the rest of the community by succeeding.

This competitive reality is equally present in churches. Experts in church growth affirm what we already know: Those churches with the best preaching and worship ministries, the best children's and youth programs, and the best facilities win at the expense of other fellowships. If anything, the postmodern and post-Christian culture accentuates this competition between churches. After all, each congregation is now competing for its share in a smaller "market."

Although the realities of market forces, egos, and the desire for independence encourage competition between churches, it has severe consequences for the body of Christ. The church's disunity and lack of cooperation greatly diminish Christianity's credibility in a postmodern world predisposed to rejecting metanarratives (overarching, unified stories of truth and meaning) and affirming multiple and even conflicting sources of truth. In our disunity and competitive spirit, the Christian narrative disintegrates into the static of many rival stories vying for attention.

BENEFITS OF MUTUALITY AND DEPENDENCE

Independence and freedom are to be valued, but our culture's idolization of them is unbiblical. The Bible's foundational words on community come in its first two chapters, Genesis 1–2. The dominant themes of this narrative are mutuality and dependence, two ideas that are not on the A-list in contemporary culture. The first humans are created with a profound difference—a gender difference—yet both male and female are described as made "in the image of God" (Genesis 1:27). In order for these finite creatures to understand the infinite God's image within them—in order for them to worship their Creator—their worship must be mutual. Their lives of worship and stewardship over God's creation depend on communication, the mutuality of relationship, and appropriate dependence on each other.

The theme is echoed in the retelling of the creation story in Genesis 2, which describes the loneliness of the first man before the woman is created. The passage reminds us that this loneliness is not God's intention (2:18). In the exercise of naming the animals and their mates, God demonstrates to the first man the relational and dependent nature of humanity with an obvious visual lesson on the dependent nature of creation (2:19-20). In a dramatic conclusion that provokes words of exultation (and worship!), the woman is created (2:21-23).

The totality of the Scriptures reinforces the creation narrative. We are not meant to be alone. Our calling is to contribute to God's work through interdependence and relationship with one another. In other words, we are called to missional dependence. This applies not only to individuals, but also to congregations that might be prone to compete with one another. Missional dependence could reduce the redundancy of our resources and programs and leave us space to enter the postmodern, emerging culture in unity and mutuality.

Sometimes our churches resemble me and my chainsaw. The chainsaw is high on my hierarchy of personal tools. It's convenient, efficient, and kind of fun to use. I feel strong and in control when I use a chainsaw. But each of the seven homes located on our circle owns a chainsaw—and none of us uses this tool more than once or twice a year. Why do we have so many chainsaws? Ignoring our affluence for the moment, part of the answer lies in the suburban "holy grail" of independence. We want to be able to use the chain-saw at the precise moment we choose, and we don't want to depend on anyone else's graciousness to tend to our little corner of creation. It's our way of being Adam in the garden and saying to Eve, "I don't need you!"

An abbreviated list of "chainsaws" in the tool sheds of many churches could include our children's programs, youth programs, support groups, mission endeavors, facilities, and vehicles. These can all be necessities, but often they are redundancies created in competition with other churches. Missional proximity and missional dependence are closely related. When congregations have a stronger sense of missional proximity, it will diminish redundancies and increase their dependence on one another. A sense of proximity encourages each congregation to develop programs and invest resources toward missional necessities in a particular community. This same sense of proximity can foster mutuality and partnership among churches in a specific ministry environment and discourage the development of redundant ministries that are already well represented in other churches.

The trajectory of the modern church in the West has been toward an obsessive individualism and the interiorization of faith as a personal practice. But this is changing amid the coming of a postmodern culture that yearns desperately for community. The effectiveness of any church's entrance into the emerging culture will be characterized, at least in part, by its ability to moderate the impact of individualism in community formation.

Transition in Mission

A lay leader in our church came by my office to borrow a key, but asked with interest about an emerging culture initiative our pastoral team was then proposing. I gave what I thought was a succinct description of our plans and dreams, but somewhere in the middle of my reply, his eyes glazed over. Instead of feigning understanding, he stated, "I really don't understand much of what you're talking about. But I trust you and hope you accomplish these dreams." As he grabbed the key and scurried off, I was left contemplating another conversation about emerging culture ministry that somehow didn't fully connect.

The truth is that the language of the emerging culture, even when it isn't perceived as threatening or deviating from orthodoxy, is often obscure for those who have little experience in this conversation. The collisions of the modern and postmodern worlds and the growth of the emerging culture leads to a cross-cultural context with much confusion and little common language. When we talk about "entering into a narrative," "embodiment of ethics," and "post-rational trajectories of discernment," we're begging for some honest confusion. But even when the insider-speak of the emerging culture is avoided, there is still a measure of disconnected communication—even here in a university community like Chapel Hill/Durham.

The existing church's journey into the emerging culture begs for a practical and common language to discuss and explore the claims of emerging church leaders and the passions of the emerging culture. In our congregation, we've found it most effective to talk about missional transition. In times when changes in spiritual formation may seem ethereal, new directions in community formation appear overly idealistic, and new paradigms of theology sound revolutionary or unorthodox, the language and practical examples of missional transition have spoken with clarity and passion in our congregation. Before describing some specific initiatives we've undertaken, let's explore the contours and parameters of missional transition.

A POISONED WELL? A CONTEXT FOR CHANGE

Oscar Muiru, Senior Pastor of Nairobi Chapel in Nairobi, Kenya, is an astute observer of American culture. He is keenly aware of the impact of U.S. culture on the gospel our churches write about, teach, and export in mission. About five years ago, I visited Nairobi and attended an informal dialogue on mission, which was also attended by several East African ministry leaders. During the meeting, Muiru commented on the African church's near obsession with replicating Western church models of education, communication, biblical exegesis, and church organization. Another leader added that the African church has drunk from the well of the U.S. church far too often without considering whether it's a poisoned well. I knew he intended neither malice nor disrespect. This pastor has a profound respect for Western missions and traces his own conversion to Western missionary efforts. But his honesty was a strong reminder that the Western church is in need of both greater cultural self-reflection and a significant transition in its understanding of mission.[89] This change in vision for mission is highly related to and consistent with the kind of transitions necessary for the church to enter into the emerging culture with authenticity and voice.

Later that same day, Muiru and one of his senior staff pastors, Murithi Wanjau, pulled me aside to reply personally to our church's invitation to come to Chapel Hill and speak at a similar dialogue on the future of mission. Muiru and Wanjau, who are very familiar with our church and have visited many times, felt they needed to respond with a polite "yes, but not right now" to this specific invitation. Muiru gently explained that if he spoke honestly on this subject, he feared he'd offend too many people whom he loved deeply. He felt our church was not yet ready to hear an African perspective on mission and to embrace a new paradigm for the mission of the church. But he did offer a series of challenges that our congregation has taken to heart.

Five years later, along with other mission leaders in our community, we began co-sponsoring a series of annual mission dialogues. Muiru has not only spoken at these events, but also preached in

---

[89] This transition has begun. I am often enthused to hear mission leaders reflect on the future. This warning about "a poisoned well" echoes similar concerns about individualism, consumerism, pragmatism, U.S. nationalism, and the reduction of the gospel to media-appropriate sound bites. See the sections in chapter 2 (on cultural intrusion and adaptation of the gospel message) for a more complete discussion of these issues.

our weekly worship services with great boldness and honesty about the future of mission from a non-Western perspective. His sermons have been received with overwhelming enthusiasm. What a difference five years can make!

What were Oscar Muiru's challenges to us? What are the missional transitions the church must consider as it moves into a postmodern, emerging culture? They include a change in the posture of mission, a re-integration of ministry to combat some classic mission reductions, a new temporal frame of reference, and a change in our cultural perspective.

Challenge 1: Breaking Down the Compartmentalization of Mission

Perhaps the most fundamental change involves a change in mindset about mission activity. The church has typically thought of missions as a series of specific activities undertaken by a uniquely trained group of individuals who work to spread the gospel as professional missionaries. Instead, we must begin to think of mission as the posture of persons seeking to perpetually participate in God's work. This redefinition breaks down a series of categories: that mission work is a set of particularly sacred activities that can be distinguished from less sacred activities, that mission work is reserved for a special class of spiritually mature persons, and that mission activities are the linear result of doctrinal and theological study. This change of perspective is often represented in contemporary missiological literature and emerging church writings by reference to the "mission" of the church, rather than the more traditional language of "missions."

The importance of this missing *s* should not be underestimated. It represents not only a breaking down of the traditional compartments of mission, but also a new identity for the church. In his writing on the missional church, George Hunsberger explains that the transformation from missions to mission accompanies a shift from understanding the church as either a location of sacred activity or an institution that produces spiritual products to viewing it as a body of people which embraces God's mission and lives in perpetual commitment to it.[90] This revolutionary shift has become the epicenter of the emerging church's identity, and many have explored its missiology in great detail.[91]

The change from *missions* to *mission* is absolutely essential for ministry transition into the emerging culture. In past eras, where Christianity was assumed as the primary worldview, the church could be a locus of sacred activity—the culture sought out the church for spiritual meaning.[92] Even as the predominance of Christianity began to fade in late modernity and early postmodernity, our society was filled with enough persons with a Christian background that a well-marketed programmatic approach to spirituality could still be highly effective in reaching the consumer-driven culture. But the effectiveness of these approaches is greatly diminished in an increasingly postmodern world that questions the ethics of Christianity and the simple goodness of Christian institutions.

A missional approach that emphasizes Christianity as a life practice and embodiment of God's redemptive work and message stands to be more authentic in our contemporary culture. Such an understanding is consistent with the historical narrative of Christianity and the life of the early church. In a society that experiences intense boredom, loneliness, and deep-seated individualism, the creation of churches as missional communities offers disconnected individuals opportunities for meaning and involvement. Furthermore, in developing this more integrated expression of Christian mission, we will eliminate some classic reductions and produce a much more integrated expression of Christian mission.

Challenge 2: Integrating Global and Local Initiatives

In the last couple of centuries, two classic reductions have plagued the Western church's understanding of mission. First, Christian conversation about mission has tended to focus on strategies and methods of international, personal evangelism.[93] Second, "missions" has

---

[90] George R. Hunsberger and Craig Van Gelder (editors), *The Church Between Gospel and Culture* (Grand Rapids, Mich.: Wm. B. Eerdmans, 1996), 337-346.

[91] To get a better idea of how we describe this change in our context, see "Where Did the S Go?" by going to *www. biblechurch.org*. Click on Mission (found in the Ministries pull-down menu) and then Values to locate this article.

[92] See also chapter 8 and particularly Rodney Clapp's explanation on Constantinian Christianity. During the Constantinian era, where Christianity enjoyed a favored status in Western culture, the church could simply throw out a welcome mat and expect to be engaged by the culture.

been understood primarily as an initiative of the Western European and North American church to the rest of the world.

Understanding the source of these reductions helps explain why they must be changed for the church to minister effectively in the emerging culture. The Western domination and orientation of mission is yet another result of Constantinianism. When the church and its theology were dominant within society and allied with its power structures, the church had little motivation for evangelism. Missiologist Darrell Guder writes:

> Terms like "mission" and "evangelism" were absent from the language of medieval Christian culture. European theology had not really dealt with the "missionary nature of the church" for over a thousand years... From the "Constantinianization" of Christianity in the fourth century onward, Christian mission was the outward expansion of the Christian culture that was the established religious force in Europe.[94]

As the Christian West began to colonize the rest of the world, mission—and particularly evangelism—was rediscovered, but in a form that was deeply influenced by colonialism. Christian travelers found vast regions with a variety of competing religions that needed evangelism. The Christian message communicated in these new evangelistic settings was also deeply entwined with the norms and characteristics of Western culture. Shaped by Western individualism, the gospel and mission became much more focused on personal salvation. With increasing secularization (as power structures became less interested in Christianity and Christian endorsement), the gospel and mission focused even more on eternity and life after death.

Guder asserts that the church has been largely unconscious of these reductions and the way they have rooted and grown throughout the history of the Western church. He notes that an understanding of the church's mission as individualistic, otherworldly, and

---

[93] Often mission activities are defined as evangelism and ministries that support evangelism.

[94] Darrell L. Guder, *The Continuing Conversion of the Church* (Grand Rapids, Mich.: Wm. B. Eerdmans, 2000), 9.

Western has particularly thrived in the evangelical wing of the U.S. church. In the late nineteenth century, evangelicals parted company with mainline Christians, asserting the sole importance of evangelism over social justice as the defining expression of missions.[95]

Guder minces no words in asserting the need to move beyond these reductions:

> My thesis is that our particular Western reductionisms are the great challenge that the North Atlantic churches face when they seek to develop a theology of evangelistic ministry…It is a question of the church's radical conversion from a deeply engrained reductionism whose result is a gospel that is too small.[96]

There are tragic consequences to this reductionism. Missions understood in this manner export large measures of Western culture enmeshed in the gospel message. This can be "the poisoned well" that the pastors in East Africa wonder about and fear. Our mission efforts can transport consumerism, competition, and individualism—values deeply antagonistic not only to the gospel but to cultures that venerate family, tradition, and dependence on community as a way of life. In nations still shaped by the shame of colonialism, a strategy that emphasizes Western initiative (and even Western superiority) can disempower national churches and national leaders. When the Western church insists on maintaining the primary initiative in missions, we expend significant resources attempting to minister in places where we have little or no credibility. This is particularly true when we send persons from our affluent culture to speak the gospel and offer solutions in areas of intense suffering.

Mission, as a Western-oriented program of personal evangelism, can also be a poisoned well for ministry in the emerging culture. A Western-dominated perspective on mission that emphasizes the international, individual, and eternal aspects of the gospel at the expense of the gospel's local, community, and present-tense attributes can be irrelevant, incomprehensible, and even offensive to postmodern and emerging culture persons.

---

[95] For a description of this parting of ways, see George Marsden, *Fundamentalism and American Culture* (New York: Oxford University Press, 1980), 85-93.

[96] Guder, 102.

Years ago when I was a youth pastor in Chapel Hill, a national collegiate ministry sponsored an evangelistic program on the campus of the University of North Carolina. Since many high school students attended this event, I was asked to host a follow-up event for teens. The speaker at this second event offered a traditional "evangelical" presentation of the gospel that emphasized making "a personal commitment to Jesus as your Lord and Savior" as a prerequisite to "eternal salvation." In the question-and-answer after the talk, many teens asked questions about environmentalism, social justice, and unity in the Christian community. I could see their increasing frustration when the speaker expressed little interest or background on these topics.

As the formal program ended, we transitioned into the inevitable pizza dinner and time of casual conversation. A group of teens approached me and asked where they could recycle the plastic drink bottles and what they should do with "these" (indicating the Styrofoam plates we'd used). When I admitted we'd given no thought to these environmental concerns in our planning, one of the kids gave me the classic look of teenage dismissal and then said to her friends, "Why are we still here?" Our incomplete gospel presentation had offended these teens and our lack of sensitivity to one of their significant moral values had reinforced their critical presuppositions against Christianity.

Our mission reductions can also be deeply frustrating and demoralizing within the church. Years ago, our church's mission programs focused almost entirely around information, prayer, and care for a group of international missionaries working in evangelistic programs. Occasionally, these missionaries would come speak at our church and those events were attended enthusiastically by a small group of the most joyful, grateful, and faithful Christians I've ever met. Yet, the limited and dwindling attendance was discouraging for several key leaders of this group. One in particular confessed to me that he was deeply disappointed that so few persons in our congregation had any interest in mission. But his discouragement was rooted in a highly specific understanding of mission.

At the time the vision and programs of several of our primary affinity groups in the church were oriented around mission experiences. Some in our fellowship were living intentionally in poor urban neighborhoods as an expression of mission. We had established a number of new social programs that were being supported with unprecedented enthusiasm. We had deacons and other fiscal leaders concerned that we weren't spending enough money on missional endeavors (especially social programs), despite a large mortgage and a tight budget. But none of these passions and energies qualified as "mission" in this person's mind.

These same reductions can also marginalize involvement and detach mission from daily living. When mission is viewed as the work of highly trained church professionals, the average Christian can feel underprepared and unequipped for mission. Focusing solely on evangelism in mission emphasizes a particular gift set, but continues to disconnect many from mission and even alleviate some from the responsibility of living missionally. Making international mission more sacred than other expressions of mission often creates barriers between mission and the realities of daily life, between the international and the local. Granted there are many ways to support evangelism and international missions without leaving home, but this tightly defined understanding of mission produces a landing strip that is too narrow for many in our churches to find their place.

Our separation of the global from the local also damages credibility overseas. For example, how can we work for racial reconciliation overseas and make little effort in this regard in our local congregations and communities? This point is especially significant in an emerging culture that places huge importance on local contexts, stories, and meanings. This same culture reacts to the sharp fragmentation of contemporary life with a strong yearning for greater integration of values and the expression of these values. To emerging culture observers, an emphasis of international ministry that is not highly integrated and consistent with local initiatives can appear to be an extension of colonialism and the exportation of a flawed culture or theology.

Challenge 3: Adding the Immediate to the Eternal

In addition to breaking down our compartmentalization of mission and integrating global and local efforts, transition in mission also requires a change in our perspective on time, as it relates to the redemptive reign of God over creation.

As we've noted, the growing threats of a secular society and disagreements with the more liberal stream of Christianity over social justice issues have led the evangelical tribe to strongly emphasize the future kingdom at the expense of the present kingdom. This preference coincides neatly with the reduction of mission to evangelism, where the goal is to invite and persuade "lost people" into the eternal kingdom. But this preoccupation with eternity leaves out a major piece of the gospel message.

One of the challenging mysteries and tensions of Jesus' teaching involves his promise of a kingdom that seems distant and heavenly but also imminent. In his great sermon on the Mount of Olives (Matthew 24), Jesus urges his followers to vigilance, warning against premature proclamations of this future kingdom and mentioning many future events and even cataclysms that must come to pass before this long-awaited day. Yet this same Jesus tells his closest followers that some who were present would not die before they saw the kingdom emerge in power (Mark 9:1). This same tension of a present and future kingdom appears throughout the New Testament. In his first letter to the churches in Asia Minor, Peter writes of a great coming salvation being held as an inheritance in eternity (1 Peter 1:4-5). Yet only a few verses later, Peter depicts that great salvation as being presently received (1 Peter 1:9).

It's easy to see how attention to God's eternal reign at the expense of the present has shaped not only our ministry interests (evangelism over social justice), but also the target and tone of ministry. Since salvation is primarily perceived in terms of an individual's fate with God, the target of our ministry becomes individual confession and personal spiritual growth, rather than community formation. A focus on eternity alone can lead to a gnawing pessimism toward society and creation, and to a potentially arrogant insensitivity to the pains of this world. Too often we minister as if we have "the answer" in the muck of life's greatest pains and mysteries.

One of my pet peeves is watching a TV quiz show host offer contestants the answer to a missed question with a smug matter-of-factness that implies the answer is simple and obvious. Our confidence in God's eternity can produce this same smugness in our tone of ministry. But this is not a season for smug attitudes within the Christian community. The technological possibilities of this world—like genetic engineering and cloning—have outdistanced our theological reflections. The whole world faces threats of unthinkable acts of terror and ethical dilemmas that will test our faith and strain our communities to their limits. We live in a world with both boundless affluence and exponentially increasing poverty. Our Christian communities have yet to fashion bold words and bold lifestyles that respond to this polarity. I believe with the whole of my being that the Christian story gives meaning and hope to the past, present, and future human condition. But I cannot always see how the kingdom Jesus promises is being born amid the pain and struggle of our world. This mystery is what drives me to live by faith, to pray diligently, and to join others in community as we pool our hopes and experiences with God. But an arrogant confidence, a reliance on simplistic answers, and the repetition that "it all works out in eternity" makes the church appear disturbingly irrelevant and out-of-touch in this season of great doubt and uncertainty.

Mission in the emerging culture needs to address the immediate reign of God in our world and culture as much as the promised eternal kingdom of God. Changing our temporal reference point to include the present tense will dramatically transform the content, goals, and tone of our ministry. As our mission begins to embrace God's kingdom on earth, we will naturally draw near to the greatest pains, needs, and injustices of this world. It is a sad fact that many in our culture increasingly expect the church to be self-righteous, impractical, and insensitive to or wrong about the greatest issues that face our society. A missiology that seeks to build God's kingdom on this earth and to embody the graciousness and generosity of Jesus' life and ministry will do much to respond to this criticism.

Challenge 4: Building Communities of Presence, Partnership, and Multiculturalism

A few years ago, I was traveling to East Africa with a group from our church to observe the impact of the AIDS pandemic and to begin to conceptualize a response by our church. There are regions in Africa where the HIV infection rate is 33 percent, and that reality was starkly evident during our trip. Perhaps the most vivid and overwhelming scene came when we drove into Langata National Cemetery in Nairobi, Kenya. The cemetery is literally right across the road from Nairobi's game park. As we crossed the road, we crossed from the amenities targeted at wealthy tourists to reality. After a short turn on a dirt road, we came across the cemetery's gravediggers. Approximately 50 men were working in a long line, each individually digging a grave. As we rounded the corner, we saw them complete the graves they were digging. Then, without a rest, each man took a few paces forward and started digging again. A new line of 50 graves would be finished before they ended their day of labor.

It was a vivid symbol of a completely different cultural reality concerning death. At home, cemetery graves are dug individually. In this setting, death appears to be isolated, rare, and sanitized by use of machinery that completes the task quickly. At Langata, the gravediggers work perpetually in large groups to keep up with the lethal devastation of AIDS. Death presents itself as human, vast, arduous, and tragic. The cultural frame of reference makes all the difference in considering the many realities of human loss.

Mission is an extension of not only theology, but also culture. Our cultural perspectives shape our mission programs and goals. As Guder described, when the epicenter of Christianity was in Western Europe, and later also in North America, it was easy to see mission as an extension of industrial and relatively affluent Western culture. From this vantage point, underdeveloped economic systems coincided with underdeveloped spirituality in other parts of the world. Mission inevitably became enmeshed in the national ambitions, paternalism, and altruism of the colonial era. This waning cultural perspective still affects our goals in mission. It's still common for U.S. Christians to view mission as efforts to charitably reach out to spiritually dark and economically depressed cultures. From this perspective mission often involves reaching out with the "magic bullets" of technology and education and the simple promise of eternal salvation.

Over the last couple of decades, the U.S. church has sought to distance itself from the simplicities of this paternalistic approach. But we are still captive to a variety of cultural perspectives that shape our mission efforts. One primary challenge is the affluence that insulates many of us from some of life's harshest realities. Many Americans live in manicured (and maybe gated) subdivisions that shout of isolation, comfort, control, and safety. Granted, these ideals are mirages. But they guide our mission efforts toward the isolation and safety of financial giving at a distance, as well as a focus on results that reflect our culture.

As pastors and church leaders, we constantly strive against and contend with this cultural captivity of mission. In our fellowship, we've tried to address this issue by promoting a mission mindset of presence, partnership, and multiculturalism. The importance of such an approach was obvious during the first few hours of our trip to Kenya to consider our congregation's response to HIV/AIDS. Jetlagged and exhausted after more than a day of travel, we met the other half of our mission team—Kenyans from several churches. Among them was Jackie, an amazing woman who had just buried her husband and was faced with the daunting task of raising five kids alone. In the midst of our initial greeting, Jackie asked us point-blank how we imagined ourselves to be "relevant" to the suffering of her country. Our team, made up of artists, graduate students, and professors—all of us Caucasian, most from upper middle-class backgrounds—took in a long, collective breath. Our initial answer was that we had no clue how we could be relevant, but that we were "here" to help.

Our team of artists and thinkers had been formed intentionally with the goal of communicating to our own culture (through a variety of mediums) the devastation that AIDS has brought upon Africa. Over the next month, we refined our reply only a bit. We realized we weren't responding to a call to be relevant. We had little to offer in that vein. But we believed our presence with those who were in pain and our desire to communicate about the calamity of AIDS was an act of faithfulness and solidarity. It was right for us to enter the pains and needs that could seem distant to us.

This lesson is not unique to our church. Experiences like this throughout the Christian community have helped forge a new missiology of presence—the repetitive faithfulness of drawing near to the pains, injustices, and needs of our world. This missiology is a commitment to be humble listeners, learners, and friends to our world, rather than privileged and benevolent problem-solvers and answer-givers. This missiology demands and employs the full range of hospitality—both receptivity and honesty—described earlier in chapter 6. It frees us to share the great narrative of God's redemption through Christ across the boundaries of comfort and culture. It also ensures that the grand God-story will be applied to the needs and hurts of our world with humility, concern, kindness, and with awareness that the needs of the human condition are at times beyond our knowledge.

In Matthew 5:3-4, Jesus began a great sermon with the strange words, "Blessed are the poor in spirit, for theirs is the kingdom of heaven. Blessed are those who mourn, for they will be comforted." There are many interpretations for these unexpected exhortations. But one reading is that those who suffer and mourn (and those who join them in their tears) develop a deeper understanding of the hope God offers and the redemption Jesus secures. I've always thought the gospel makes more sense when we are present to both the wounds of our world and our own woundedness. A missiology of a gentle presence and honest self-reflection can and will be a powerful catalyst to ministry in the emerging culture—a culture that seems more aware than any other about its own wounds and the failures of simplistic responses.

The missiology of partnership flows naturally from the ministry of presence and the awareness it brings to the real needs of others. Recognizing the limits of our abilities to respond to these needs, we seek to build bridges—both inside and outside the Christian community—that allow us to share the burden and to pool our knowledge and experiences in reaching out. One of the greatest criticisms the postmodern world lodges against the church is our disunity and our intentional lack of cooperation with others who care and seek to respond to the needs of our world. The credibility of the church, within the diversity and unique connectedness of our world, rests partly on our willingness to join with others who reach out. If our churches are willing to feed, clothe, advocate, and care for others only in collaboration with those who affirm our doctrine, then not only will our ministries be far less effective than they could be, but also very few will ever hear our words about the redemption God extends. Diverse partnerships and a spirit of cooperation need to become prominent attributes of our missional transition.

An extension of this commitment to partnership is a missiology of multiculturalism. One of our church's first partnership efforts was an international friendship with Nairobi Chapel in Kenya. International partnerships can be fruitful starting points for North American churches. But the distance and expense of frequent travel can also enhance a lack of accountability in these relationships. When we're far from home, it's easy to temporarily reshape our identity. For that reason, Oscar Muiru suggested that our establishing an international partnership with their congregation in Kenya would be far less fruitful and potentially not worth the effort unless our church placed a similar emphasis on local partnerships and multiculturalism. The poisonous well of racial and cultural segregation is a huge impediment for the U.S. church in ministering to the emerging culture. This desperately needs to be changed as we move into the greater diversity and heightened sensitivities of multiculturalism in the emerging culture.

Earlier in this chapter, I recounted a story where an evangelistic program for youth was discredited due to its environmental insensitivity. Today, those same teens might ask how our ministry is shaped by the huge Hispanic population explosion in North Carolina or by our relationships with the African-American majority in Durham. Multiculturalism is not a "politically correct" burden placed on the church by a liberal society. The Bible's clear description of the people of God is an "every nation church." The many possible ministry expressions of multiculturalism will be nonnegotiable essentials of the church's mission in the emerging culture.

ONE CONGREGATION'S JOURNEY OF MISSIONAL TRANSITION

As I explained earlier, missional transition has been central to our church's experience of transition into an emerging culture perspective in ministry. I believe our journey of missional transition can be helpful to others who are thinking about how to minister more effectively in the emerging culture.[97]

A Unifying Vision

In 2000, our church had many wonderful events occurring under the banner of missions. There were vibrant prayer groups meeting to support our long-term and short-term cross-cultural workers, which continue to this day. A few social justice ministries flourished. We offered regular short-term mission projects. We had a long history of ministry to the many international students who come to our local universities. But these fine ministries were a loose constellation of events. These programs shared the mission line of our budget, but there was no unifying vision.

---

[97] As I tell a bit of our story on missional transition, I want to acknowledge the friendship, partnership, inspirational leadership, visionary insight, and relentless efforts of Jim Thomas. Jim is a bivocational pastor at the Chapel Hill Bible Church. He is a professor of epidemiology at UNC's School of Public Health whose areas of interest and expertise include STDs, the social contexts of epidemics, and ethics in public health. Jim and I have been dreaming of and working together for missional transition for over a decade. Many of the transitions I describe in this chapter are the direct result of Jim's vision and leadership.

Transition into the emerging culture was undoubtedly part of our motivation for developing an overarching vision for mission. But the greater driving force was our belief that mission could be a connector and catalyst for worship, spiritual formation, and community.[98] We rightfully surmised that our fellowship was a dozing giant with great potential in mission. But it was our vision that mission could facilitate spiritual formation, worship, and community formation that inspired many to become involved. Our invitation was not only to build God's present kingdom and participate in God's work of redemption, but also to shape a Christian community that would have meaning and influence in a growing, post-Christian, and postmodern world.

The holistic intentionality of this vision has helped us to pursue a more integrated and less compartmentalized view of mission. Mission is becoming less the activity of professional, spiritual superheroes supported by a few interested cheerleaders, and more of a life posture and rule for the entire congregation. The imagined barrier between outreach and spiritual formation is eroding as more and more people in our community realize that mission as a lifestyle is inseparable from spiritual growth.[99] The barrier between mission and worship is also eroding—the understanding of mission as a life rule complements and reinforces the transition that allows us to see worship as our posture before God, rather than just a series of events.[100] Mission has become an open door of involvement for long-time Christians and those new to the journey of faith. The firewall between evangelism and social justice has been almost entirely obliterated. It seems hard to believe that only seven years ago a new young adults ministry in our church imploded in disagreement after a guest teacher placed the importance of social justice work on par with evangelism. There are few here now who would even raise an eyebrow at that assertion.

[98] Obviously all of these are arenas of emerging culture ministry transition. But, regardless of the cultural perspective driving the expression of these ministry arenas, each is a vital part of a spiritually healthy fellowship.

[99] Some have used the term "inreach" to emphasize a sharp demarcation between spiritual growth and missional activities. This sharp division inevitably encourages a linear approach that views mission as a response of faith for those who have reached a point of spiritual maturity.

[100] It's really an artificial exercise to separate missional transition from the transitions in worship, spiritual formation, and community formation. Each of these transitions involves movement from programs, measurable pragmatism, and static definitions to more holistic and integrated methods. An integrated and holistic perspective reveals the intricate connection of mission with worship, spiritual formation, and community formation.

This broad and integrated vision has also provided opportunities to participate in ministry that have gone far in demythologizing the emerging church and eliminating fears about ministry directed toward the emerging culture. So many of the theological and philosophical oversimplifications explored in the first part of this book have evaporated with solid examples of these ministry principles.

Young Adults as an Essential Affinity Group

Our vision of missional transition was initiated among our young adults first, an affinity group we deemed essential to missional transition.[101] The principles of worship, leadership, spiritual formation, community formation, and mission described in this book were foundational to the young adults ministry we began six years ago. Although the emerging culture is not an age-related or generational phenomenon, so many of our young adults either had emerging culture worldviews or were enmeshed in emerging culture relationships. They provided a ready community in which we could dialogue, dream, and even be challenged about our vision for emerging culture ministry in our specific context.[102] When we began to develop a wide range of missional possibilities, our young adults provided a large pool of enthusiastic participants. Through their passion for mission and their demonstration of the vision in action, our young adults ministry created a contagious onramp for the wider congregation's involvement in mission.

---

[101] I had led our youth ministry for almost a decade with many of the emerging culture ministry principles I've described. This was really a necessity since so many of our kids were thoroughly postmodern in their worldview. Sadly, at least in our setting, the youth ministry was a lightning rod for critique and fear. During this time of intense change, many parents wanted a ministry that resembled their own adolescent needs and youth ministry experiences. In our university-obsessed environment, the experiences of teens are constantly trumped by university events (who wants to go the high school basketball game when you might be able to see Duke or Carolina play!). This limits the ability of teens to influence the congregation. This is not the case in every church. Many of my comments about young adults could be applied to youth ministries in other settings.

[102] I don't want to imply that this is always easy. We had some young adults who preferred a traditional young adults ministry that emphasized Christian life principles, social events, social insulation for Christian young adults, and segmentation from the greater body. But we felt a great freedom to take this path because we were building a new ministry and because we were enthusiastic about many other young adult ministries in neighboring churches. Our sense of community and noncompetitive partnership with other fellowships (who offered more traditional young adult ministries) offered some security in taking this risk. I would not operate an affinity group with a different ministry philosophy than the rest of a church in perpetuity. Ultimately, there must be synergy between the affinity and the rest of the church or you are just sowing seeds of conflict! I will comment more on affinity group strategies in chapter 10.

Mission Partnerships

The beating heart of our missional transition has been a series of ministry partnerships. Partnership as a methodology breaks down the sense of independence that limits community formation. The different experiences and perspectives of diverse partners remind us of our own finitude and prepare us to worship an infinite God. Partnerships provide opportunities to practice the hospitality that transforms our spiritual formation and opens us to missional transition as we become aware of the wounds and needs of our neighbors and our inability to provide easy answers.

Our congregation has been stretched, taught, prophetically challenged, humbled, and embraced by a series of wonderful partnerships:

- Our international partnership with Oscar Muiru and the Nairobi Chapel family has obliterated any sense of Western preeminence in mission. Their vision for ministry and willingness to take risks has often far exceeded our own.[103] Their prophetic voice rings out in parts of the world where we lack credibility and welcome, and offers an essential critique of our ministry and cultural context that we never could have seen ourselves. Most recently, Kyama and Wambui Mugambi have joined our staff as a visiting pastor family, continuing Nairobi Chapel's gift of cross-cultural challenge and prophetic insight into our ministry.

- Our friendship with Nairobi Chapel led to another partnership that has had a powerful impact on our community. Nairobi Chapel member Jane Wathome had a dream of inspiring churches to join together in ministry and offer healthcare, companionship, and economic development support to those affected by HIV/AIDS and their families in Nairobi. She founded Beacon of Hope[104], a warm community that teaches the skill of rug-making to women

[103] Humorously, Oscar preached in Chapel Hill the very day we announced an emerging culture mission in neighboring Durham. As he casually described Nairobi Chapel's challenge to their congregants to plant churches in other continents, our mission seven miles away did not seem so adventurous or risky!

[104] See www.beaconafrica.org

affected by HIV/AIDS, offers a safe space for friendship and work, holds daily worship gatherings, and provides an extensive and nutritious daily meal to these women and their children. When our congregation was asked to join in the founding of this ministry, we jumped in with two feet.[105] In addition to regularly selling the Beacon of Hope rugs, our community members have sponsored a variety of fundraisers, ranging from yard sales to weekend music festivals. This partnership has pushed the missional transition of mission as a life posture and rule to the forefront of our community. We've been delighted whenever numerous other U.S. churches—locally and nationally—have joined with us in these efforts. We continue to learn from the missional experiences of other churches while collaborating with the ministry of Beacon of Hope.

- Oscar Muiru's challenge that we establish a partnership with a local African-American church was realized when the Rev. Michael Page and the Antioch Baptist Church in Durham graciously welcomed us into a friendship. This partnership has been cemented by the formation of a joint community-development nonprofit and numerous shared ministries. Durham is a city with a rich African-American heritage, a majority African-American population, and a history scarred by intense racial polarization. This friendship has forced us to constantly confront the portion of our cultural captivity marked by racial fears and segregation.

- In the past couple of years, we've pursued ministry partnerships with Duke Divinity School. One of the many burgeoning fruits of this effort has been collaboration and the mutual support of faculty members of the South American Theological Seminary in Brazil. Although Duke is a renowned and respected divinity school, this partnership was controversial within our fellowship. From the vantage point of our evangelical roots, some view Duke as a "liberal institution" and as "the other team." This partnership confronts this prejudice and challenges us to move missionally

---

[105] One of my most memorable days in ministry included being at the Beacon of Hope for a time of worship and then watching the first group of women who were served by this ministry receive their first paychecks for their labors!

beyond the liberal/conservative cold war (a missional must in the emerging culture).

- Other significant partnerships include ministry in the Guanajuato region of Mexico (a territory that is home to many of the Hispanic immigrants in our community), a relationship with InterVarsity Christian Fellowship (particularly its Emerging Culture Project led by Jimmy Long), and a long friendship with Emergent. This partnership with Emergent was particularly well chosen, since that group's vision of emergent culture ministry was quite alien and even frightening to our congregation in the mid-1990s. Our community's willingness to invest time, money, and other resources in this visionary organization has stretched and supported our identity and ability to dream.

Multiethnicity and Diversity

In our observations of the mission efforts of other fellowships, it often seemed as if many churches made a choice: Either they'd seek to build ethnically diverse partnerships with other congregations or they'd work consciously and actively toward achieving multiethnicity within their own congregation. Our desire was to eliminate the either/or of these goals and make it a *both/and* instead. Our fellowship has never been completely homogenous in its ethnicity. The diversity of our area certainly gave us more opportunities than many churches to be diverse, but our diversity lacked intentionality and was very inconsistently expressed. Our hope was that the partnerships we established would both draw us into multiethnic relationships and inspire multiethnicity within our congregation. This is certainly a long journey, but it has begun and we are beginning to see some fruits of this desire.

Pastor Jim Thomas has pointed out that our vision for international student ministry has been a catalyst for this transformation. We've always given significant resources and attention to ministry to internationals and international students. But we made a conscious shift from having a ministry "to" internationals to a ministry "among" internationals. One important first step involved adding internationals and racial diversity to our cross-cultural committee. This move toward diversity in leadership guided us to many other expressions of this changed philosophy, including adding room on our staff and elder board for a visiting international pastor, adding multicultural art to the décor of our facility, and embracing multicultural languages, stories, and songs in our worship.

Our annual missional gathering, Catalyst, has strayed far from the traditional "bring home our missionaries and send out more missionaries" model. Under Jim's leadership (and that of our now very diverse leadership team), Catalyst was birthed as a multi-church gathering led by international leaders focusing on the concerns and passions of these leaders from other cultures. These dialogues not only stretch us beyond our American cultural perspective, but they also further motivate us to discover the delights of multiethnic fellowship. Like many other churches that share the sensitivity of multiethnicity, we acknowledge that much more growth is needed in this arena. We eagerly look forward to continuing along this journey.

The Power of Missional Transition

Our story of missional transition is paralleled by many other fellowships that are walking some of these same paths, as well as exploring trails we've not yet considered. I don't intend for our congregation's narrative to be copied as a template, to be assumed to be unique, or to be presumed to be easy and matter-of-fact at every point. In fact, some of the changes we've experienced have been painful and extremely challenging.

Among the realizations we value most is the recognition of the strong parallels between missional transition and emerging culture ministry transition. The church's sometimes unwittingly and uncritical entrenchment of message and method in modernity is highly related to the occasional poisoned well of our ministry internationally. The transition of the church into the emerging culture coincides significantly with the conversion of the church in mission and evangelism that Darrel Guder seeks.[106]

We've experienced missional transition as an exciting pathway to embracing a new identity as a church in a radically transformed cultural context. We also deeply value the understanding that missional transition can be an effective language, a powerful example, and a contagious motivator of allied transitions in spiritual formation, leadership, and community formation. In the next chapter, we'll return to the question of how this journey into the emerging culture can shape the church's worship life.

[106] Guder, 102.

Transition in Worship: "So What about Worship, Anyway?"

Earlier in the book, I challenged the notion that the existing church's transition into the emerging culture should be focused on a redesign and reprogramming of its worship services. In fact, I argued that the worship service was very much the wrong place to start when thinking about emerging culture ministry. But I did promise I'd return to the topic of worship and make some specific comments.

Actually, I'd contend that I've *already* included a great deal of material about worship, for I believe worship, when properly understood, is inextricably linked to spiritual formation, church leadership, community formation, and mission. This becomes more obvious as we consider the creation story in Genesis and other biblical portraits of the nature of worship.

WORSHIP IN THE BIBLICAL NARRATIVES

The first two chapters of Genesis, the book of origins, reveal that a primary motivation for God's creative work is the establishment of a community of worshippers. Genesis opens with the assumption of an omnipotent and preexistent Creator: "In the beginning God created…" (Genesis 1:1). The formation of humanity on the sixth day places human beings within the much larger context of the universe's creation, yet also paints humanity as the culmination of that creation (Genesis 1:26-31). Made "in the image of God" (Genesis 1:27), men and women are able to know and relate to God, and thus they are created for a worship relationship that is natural for finite creations of an infinite Creator. The charge given to humanity in Genesis 1:28—to "be fruitful," "fill," "subdue," and "rule"—is a special and privileged task of worship. Designed with the capacity to know their Creator, humanity is called to a loving representation of God's purpose in the world. These tasks are comprehensive, involving the whole of their being.

Humanity's task of worship is to be accomplished in community. God's formation of humanity in two distinct genders reminds us that a fuller understanding of the presence, experience, and image of God requires friendship, community, and communication. This essential point is resoundingly affirmed in Genesis 2:18 when God observes, "it is not good for the man to be alone." In the goodness of creation, which is repetitively affirmed in this narrative, this declaration of incompleteness booms out like a thunderous shout. To truly know God and to reflect the character of God in worship, relationships are essential. As I stated in a previous chapter, there is no isolated "personal faith" outside of community.

Community teaches us that we are finite (since we don't share or even understand all the experiences of our community) and gently reminds us to worship God who is indeed infinite and is able to relate intimately with all of creation. The ultimate description of a community in worship comes in the final words of this text, as the first man and woman are portrayed as naked and without shame (Genesis 2:25). They are united and dependent on God and each other.

The story of creation reveals worship as the intended function and essential identity of humanity. Our worship is to be perpetual, holistic, and communal. In the New Testament—despite the movement of the great narrative of God's redemption through the events of Jesus' incarnation and resurrection, the coming of the Spirit at Pentecost, and the birth of the church—a similar vision of worship remains. A key text is Romans 12:1-2:

> Therefore, I urge you, brothers, in view of God's mercy, to offer your bodies as living sacrifices, holy and pleasing to God—this is your spiritual act of worship. Do not conform any longer to the pattern of this world, but be transformed by the renewing of your mind. Then you will be able to test and approve what God's will is—his good, pleasing and perfect will.

Here the rich images of sacrifice, drawn from Old Testament worship rituals, form the background of a strong reinforcement of worship as a holistic life expression, which includes bodily sacrifice, intellectual renewal, and countercultural living. Moving through the New Testament, we find a great many examples of worship, but very few prescriptions as to how this worship should be organized.[107] The emphasis is on the totality and perpetuity of worship expression, rather than its forms.

WORSHIP TRANSITION: RULE AND POSTURE OVER PROGRAM

The biblical traditions remind us that worship is more than the church services we attend. The relationship of the created to the Creator must be more. It's more than the bands or orchestras, testimonies or media pieces, expositions or sermons, sacraments or ordinances, formal liturgies or impromptu prayers, or any other elements of our worship gatherings. This simple truth is too often forgotten in many of our traditions.

Worship is the intended posture of all humans—and all of creation—in relationship to an infinite Creator. Our lives of worship naturally include our words (and our inner speech), our emotions, our thoughts, our actions, and our relationships. Worship is a rule of life in acknowledgement of God's existence, goodness, and purposes. It's the orientation of our whole selves to God's presence, the community expression of God and God's kingdom.

Understanding worship in this manner really shouldn't require any transition at all. But I believe this is the transition the church needs most as it enters the emerging culture. We live in a culture that encourages fragmentation and compartmentalization, ripping our daily living apart from our spiritual convictions. We are emerging from a theologically reinforced, modern consensus that exalts individualism (over community), objective realities (over the subjectivity of experience), the compartmentalization of life (over a holistic perspective), and scientifically validated knowledge (over beauty and mystery).

[107] Even the prescriptions of the Eucharist and baptism are not given with such clarity that a consensus emerges in regards to the practice and administration of these essentials!

Modernity, when it exploded into human consciousness, reoriented (even rescued) the church's worship from the excesses of institutional control and abuses of superstition. But after many years of dominance by thinking rooted in modernity, the Enlightenment, and a technological society, our understanding and practice of worship desperately needs to rediscover its Genesis roots.

This rediscovery is absolutely essential for the church's witness, credibility, and communication in an emerging culture that strongly critiques the residual marks of modernity on spiritual exploration and understanding. The good news is that this rediscovery seems to be occurring everywhere.

I remember vividly my first visit to the Ekklesia community in Houston, Texas, back in 2002. After several years of friendship and partnership with pastor Chris Seay, I was aware of his passion for whole-life worship and the integration of art, beauty, and mystery into the worship expression of Christian community. Nonetheless, I was amazed by both the quality and utilization of art in their community's meeting space. I wondered aloud how long it might take for existing churches to follow the lead of creative, apostolic communities like Ekklesia. The answer: not very long!

Though still far from the passion and intentionality that Ekklesia places on mutual forms of artistic expression, the existing church is beginning to follow their lead. That same year I visited Ekklesia, our church opened a brand new facility with a large, warm, well-lit foyer. Our initial impulse was to fill the walls with information and programmatic opportunities. But after a process of passionate negotiation, we decided to cover these walls with creations made by artists in our church and community. Works of art also began to creep onto the stage of our auditorium. The change in our worship space led to changes in activity. Traditional programs began to yield to art walks, experiential worship events, and greater utilization of the many musicians in our community.

Today, local singer/songwriters, a wide array of bands and musicians, and the North Carolina Symphony all use our auditorium regularly. We consider it an essential part of our mission to host and patronize these events. This path has produced new experiences of worship for us and has expanded our vocabulary of worship. The absence of these artistic expressions would be immediately noticed and mourned. I offer this account not to illustrate our great uniqueness and creativity, but because this is becoming a common evolution among churches in our culture—even churches like ours that once tended to think of music primarily as a prelude to teaching.

The point is not to start ripping down your bulletin boards, redesigning your worship spaces, recruiting painters and sculptors to create during your sermons, and reconceiving your existing worship programs. Any of these approaches might be a fine idea—but they also could comprise yet another orchestrated and programmatic approach to worship transition that would miss the real point. The real key is to rediscover worship as a posture and rule of life that acknowledges and embodies the character of God and the purposes of God's redemptive kingdom.

THE PATH OF WORSHIP TRANSITION

Of course, worship transition will have programmatic implications. New worship services may be created and a few bulletin boards might meet untimely ends. But the comprehensive worship transition I am recommending is much more than a programmatic innovation or new methodology. I believe an expanded understanding of worship—shaped by God's creative intent in Genesis and Paul's theology in Romans—can guide us on this journey and keep us from reducing worship transition to programmatic change.

Do you remember the Venn diagrams we used in high school chemistry and mathematics, which included universal sets and a range of subsets? Using this metaphor, worship is the universal set; spiritual formation, community formation, and mission are all subsets of worship. Our efforts to create new leadership structures should also be motivated by the impulse to worship. Creating a community that reflects God's character, embodies God's purposes, and proclaims God's gracious invitation to redemption is ultimately an expression of worship; a living out of our desire to respond to God's creative intent in forming a community of worshippers.

We should also note that these new patterns of life cannot be divorced from theological reflection. The practices of the church or, perhaps more properly, the worship of the church in the emerging culture are informed by and also inform new epistemologies and theological explorations available to us in this new season. Hence, I believe that all that has come before this chapter is part of worship transition.

The church's transition into the emerging culture is truly a corporate, holistic, and comprehensive reorientation of our understanding of worship. This reorientation is a rediscovery of God's creative design and the church's historical understanding of worship, as well as the embodiment of God's creative intent in a vastly changed culture.

In the final chapter, we'll explore six Old Testament images that can offer us support and guidance on this journey.

CHAPTER ELEVEN

The Journey into the Emerging Culture

God's first recorded words to Abraham in Genesis 12:1-3 were a call to the transitions, fears, discomforts, and unknowns of a distant journey: "Leave your country, your people and your father's household and go." This call to an unknown future came to Abraham with a three-fold promise. Along the journey, Abraham was promised God's continued presence ("I will show you"), an extraordinary experience of community ("I will make you into a great nation") and a missional blessing ("I will bless you; I will make your name great, and you will be a blessing…and all peoples on earth will be blessed through you"). This Scripture has great relevance for the church as we sit on the threshold of the emerging culture.

The Christian community faces the discomforts and unknowns of new theological and philosophical conversations—conversations that stray from the familiar questions and answers raised by modernity. It's likely we'll form communities and structures vastly different from those most familiar to us. I strongly believe the journey will require continuing conversion in order for the church to become a universal and missional blessing in the future. The existing church's long history of adaptation shouts these hopes, and the early fruitfulness of the emerging church whispers this eventuality. Most of all, through Scripture and history, the church is assured of the continued presence of God's Spirit as it travels to new lands.

As I've considered the existing church's journey into emerging culture, several images from the journey of Abraham and the nation God formed from him have inspired me. My thoughts have been drawn to three historic images from this narrative—the cities of refuge and sanctuary in Israel, the temple of Israel, and the tents of the tabernacle. I've also reflected on three gatherings of God's people: the tents of family and community life, the tribes into which the Israelites were grouped, and the nation composed of many diverse tribes. I believe these six images offer a helpful framework in considering the church's potential pathways into the emerging culture.

CITIES OF REFUGE AND SANCTUARY: DIALOGICAL PATHS

In Numbers 35, the Israelites camp in the land of Moab by the Jordan River as they prepare to dwell in the land promised to them by Yahweh. God commands them to designate six cities of refuge within the land allotted for the community of priests. In a culture with a developing judicial system built on personal vengeance, these cities provided a place of due process for murderers, opportunity for restitution for those who'd hurt others, and sanctuary for the innocent. Since this land was given to the Levites, or priests, the religious establishment and the judicial system merged in this gracious provision.

I believe conversations about emerging culture ministry will inevitably produce the genius of new theological constructs and the gift of new ministry practices. But these same dialogues will encourage some heretical felonies and more than a few inadvertent misdemeanors. We must provide safe places of refuge and sanctuary where these conversations and reflections can occur.

Among the greatest joys I've had in working with Emergent and its organizational forebears are the opportunities we've created for ministry leaders and spiritual travelers to gather in community for short seasons of refuge, reflection, and exploration. In these gatherings, we've heard countless stories of pioneers and leaders with new questions and sensitivities who were wearied and bruised by their experiences in existing churches. Persons on a spiritual journey or leaders who are reenvisioning ministry regularly contact Emergent and its allied organizations when looking for this safe space.

At a recent Emergent gathering, I welled up with tears of joy as I spoke with a friend who was celebrating a new marriage, an exciting new missional job, and the blessing and affirmation of his creativity and leadership in the Christian community. When I'd met him two years earlier, he'd just been fired from the staff of a large, prominent church. He was tired, grieved, and wounded. Providentially, he received a gracious welcome into an emerging church community where his story was heard, his wounds were embraced, and his thoughts and gifts were welcomed. He found a community of refuge.

The church's entrance into the emerging culture requires an insistent intentionality in creating safe places for dialogue, creative reflection, and experimental practices. The forms for these sanctuaries can be very diverse. In some communities, they will take the form of programs like worship services, affinity groups, and traditional classes. In others, book discussions, media groups, online communities, and other informal gatherings will meet this need. The specifics of these safe places are less important than the will to create and protect them.

Providing places of safety are essential if we would engage in the kinds of theological dialogue recommended in chapters 2–4. When these creative sanctuaries and refuges do not develop, it's often because communities don't value dialogue or they're willing to settle for simplifications or fearful generalizations rather than exploring beyond them.

In my own ministry journey, I'm so thankful for the unique value placed on dialogue in our fellowship and for the egalitarian leadership that fosters this value. Jim Abrahamson, our founding pastor, insisted that our conservative church must have a liberal learning style and a gracious ministry style. Our elders insisted on hiring some staff and welcoming elders whose perspectives differed from the mainstream of our fellowship.

I am particularly thankful for one of our perennial elders, Norman Acker, who has embodied this value splendidly. Norman and I are quite different: we are on opposite ends of the political spectrum; his kids have been home-schooled, while our children have been in the public schools; our families choose different extracurricular activities; and our theological beliefs also vary. But as an elder and a regular chair of our board, Norman has valued an emerging culture exploration and has continually protected this conversation. He recently introduced me to a class of skeptics by confessing that he'd often found my ministry passions to be a bit alien or confusing. But he stuck with the conversation for years and has become a strong advocate for making a seat at the table for emerging culture thought and practice.

Keith Newell is another great friend to appropriate dialogue in our fellowship. Like Norman, Keith is a perennial elder. Keith is a persistent agent of reconciliation, listening, and community in our church. He weeps when someone separates from our church while wounded or in anger. When he stumbles on rumors, gossip, and brokenness due to poor communication, he insists on dialogue and volunteers seemingly endless amounts of time to be a gentle presence in these conversations.[108] I lurked in awe during an online conversation he had with an angry congregant who'd sent a very critical e-mail to our entire church directory. Keith demonstrated an ability to hear the critique, but he also helped this congregant see that while "venting" might be an American entitlement, it wasn't a biblically protected right. On more than a few occasions, Keith has blunted the impact of my own poor communication about emerging culture ministry by encouraging conversations that helped to short-circuit misunderstandings or accusations.

Creating these sanctuaries for dialogue and reflection may be among the least complicated yet most essential paths into the emerging culture for the church. These places of refuge cannot be just for those inside the church. We also need to openly welcome those who reside outside the confines of the church. For these conversations to occur, churches need leaders who will promote the value of dialogue in the community and protect the spirit of dialogue in the various forms it takes.

---

[108] When I first met Keith, he won my everlasting admiration by praying in a public gathering that his own business would not grow so that it wouldn't overwhelm his family time and this ministry of listening and reconciliation!

THE JERUSALEM TEMPLE: INSTITUTIONAL PATHS

In the theocracy of Israel, the temple was a beautiful centerpiece of national pride and the locus of civil and religious authority. It was an edifice of meticulous construction and extravagant beauty (1 Kings 5–7). But most important to the religious life of Israel, the temple was the place of God's presence, the home of the ark of the covenant and the most sacred treasures of the Israelites (1 Kings 8:1-11).

Jesus affirmed the central importance of the temple. He used temple language to refer to his own body and death on the cross (John 2:19-21), and the early church applied similar language to the church (Ephesians 5:23). For Christians, the church takes on much of the symbol and role of the grand temple at Jerusalem. Just as the Israelites believed God's presence was found in the temple, the church believes God's presence is found in the community that gathers to worship God.

In times of national change and spiritual renewal, the Israelites rebuilt their temple or reformed their temple practices. While in exile, Nehemiah wept at reports of a ruined and disgraced Jerusalem without walls or a functioning temple (Nehemiah 1:1-4). When Nehemiah and Ezra led the return of the Jewish people from exile, they naturally rebuilt the temple and restored its system of sacrifices. Jesus had a profound respect for the importance of the temple to the law and religious heritage of Israel. Yet he purged the temple courts of merchants and regularly challenged the religious establishment by healing on the Sabbath (Matthew 21:12-14). His death not only shook the earth, but also resulted in a miraculous and dramatic ripping of the temple curtain that separated the holiest portion of the temple from its outer courts (Matthew 27:50-51).

The symbol of the temple in the life of Israel reminds us of the need for institutional transition if the church would enter the emerging culture. The emerging culture has raised new theological questions and has motivated the rediscovery of historic ministry practices and the exploration of new practices. But many of the pathways of adaptation in theology and practice will be blunted without corresponding institutional transition. While the necessary transitions will vary from congregation to congregation, we will need to be diligent, thoughtful, and faithful in our examination of church government, membership practices, the administration of the sacraments or ordinances, and our ecumenical relationships in this new season.

One area that will surely be an issue for many churches and parishes is the concentration of leadership and authority in a few individuals and leaders. In chapter 7, I recommended a path of transition that accentuated plurality in leadership without destroy- ing apostolic leadership. Leadership environments that encourage creative community participation and invite cultural dialogue are not necessarily antithetical to "strong" leadership. Instead, these environments can be a specific expression of strong leadership. Nevertheless, the direction and theology of so many churches is dominated by the perspective and prejudices of a single leader or a small group of leaders. This reality often creates an insensitivity or inflexibility to the opportunities and challenges of the emerging culture. Two recent experiences illustrate this point.

Not long ago, a seminary friend who serves as associate pastor of a nationally prominent church visited me. She told a sad story of obsessive control, intimidation, and accusation of the church's associate staff by the executive staff team. In this case, the "sins" of the associate staff had nothing to do with emerging culture is- sues directly. This already immense church was lagging behind its growth goals and the executive staff needed someone to blame. This church was tacitly approving a goal-driven leadership environment with little or no sensitivity to cultural change. I fear this scene will be repeated regularly as our culture drifts toward postmodernity and a post-Christian milieu. It will become increasingly difficult for churches to reach growth goals, even as the mechanisms to reach these goals become increasingly irrelevant to the questions and concerns of a changed culture. The image of Egyptian masters telling their Israelite slaves to make the same quota of bricks without straw comes to mind (Exodus 5:1-21).

Just two days before this conversation took place, I'd bumped into another seminary friend at the airport. He's a senior pastor who was traveling with his whole staff team. Our conversation eventually drifted to emerging culture topics. After I made a few enthusiastic assertions, the nods of my friend's team became bold, Cheshire cat grins. Finally, my friend blurted out, "These guys are constantly trying to bring up this conversation, but I've feared it was a distraction or an invitation to a theological slippery slope!" Clearly, the emerging culture conversation had begun at his church, but it hadn't quite reached the senior pastor. My friend committed to tuning into his staff and this conversation. But this very common situation creates great potential for frustration and division, as increasing numbers of staff serve with assumptions and methodologies that are alien or threatening to formal leadership in their churches.

These stories are strong reminders that institutional transition will involve sensitizing key leaders to the importance of this conversation. Cultural changes have always meant significant institutional changes within the church's practices. Jesus' interactions at the temple and with the leaders of the day serve as some inspiration to us. He affirmed, dialogued with, challenged, provoked, and confronted these leaders to recognize and embrace the gracious new paradigm that he brought. Our ability to replicate his example represents one critical path into the emerging culture.

TABERNACLE: THE PATH OF MISSIONAL COMMUNITY

Before the ark of the covenant resided in Solomon's temple, it was kept in the tabernacle. The tabernacle, though less ornate than the temple, had the same sacred significance as the dwelling place of Yahweh among the people (Exodus 40:33-35). The tabernacle was a mobile, tent structure established in the desert as the Israelites wandered between their servitude in Egypt and their occupation of the Promised Land. The tabernacle dictated the location of the community and guided them as they traveled. When the cloud that revealed God's presence stayed over the tents of the tabernacle, the Israelites camped. When the cloud lifted and moved, the people followed (Numbers 9:15-22).

The tabernacle represents a mobility and a responsiveness to God that brings to mind the way missional communities are embodying the gospel in an emerging or postmodern context. Many diverse types of gatherings fit under this broad definition, from church plants, to intentional businesses and entrepreneurial associations, to house churches, to monastic communities, to informal friendships that form around a specific mission. These communities are typically smaller (thus more mobile) and newer (thus more culturally flexible) than most established churches.

In some ways, missional communities have become the scouts of the existing church, traveling faster and far ahead of the wagon train while observing the lay of the land ahead. Apart from the larger structure, they are freer to speak their own language and do things expeditiously, while retaining some responsibility to and relationship with those who follow (hopefully).

The church has a long history of being greatly blessed by missional movements. Historical monasticism is an excellent example. In the great monastic orders, traditions of scholarship, community, mysticism, and contemplative spirituality were nurtured and protected. Even though parish life had different realities and demands, these orders had an impact on daily living and worship throughout the church.[109] In times when certain values were ignored or marginalized in the larger church, monastic communities kept them alive and fresh for future generations. The great founders of these orders would surely be delighted by the surging interest in monasticism today—particularly among Protestants. The Reformation yielded a distancing from artistic expression, mysticism, and contempla-

---

[109] I've greatly benefited from the writings and rule of St. Ignatius of Loyola. Ignatius was the founder of the Jesuit society. His Spiritual Exercises were the foundation of Jesuit spirituality and practice. Not wishing that this experience be restricted to the monastery, Ignatius wrote a 30th Annotation to his exercises to be used as a disciple of prayer by laypersons. A Jesuit spiritual director took me through this annotation of the exercises years ago. I was moved deeply by the theological acuity and practical spiritual wisdom of this now ancient work. For a contemporary version of the exercises, I recommend James W. Skehan, *Place Me With Your Son: Ignatian Spirituality in Everyday Life* (Washington D.C.: Georgetown University Press, 1991).

tive spirituality in the church. Centuries later, these treasures of the Christian tradition have been protected and refined and remain available to the spiritual nurture of the whole church.

Missional communities and established churches need one another as we move into the emerging culture. The established church has so many resources and experiences to offer to missional communities. In return, missional communities offer the larger church the intensity of community life, the freedom to take risks in missional expression and cultural engagement, and the capability to react rapidly to changing needs and new contexts.

My experiences with Beacon of Hope in Nairobi (see chapter 9) have shaped my passion regarding the importance of missional communities. When this ministry to persons infected with and affected by HIV/AIDS began in the slum of Ongata Rongai (outside Nairobi), most local churches weren't even willing to talk about AIDS, let alone offer ministry to the AIDS stricken. Watching Beacon of Hope volunteers of all social classes walk the streets of this slum to visit the sick and dying inspired many other churches to action. A few months after the Beacon of Hope was formed, I was invited to preach in one of these churches about the missional and theological implications of AIDS. When I said words like *AIDS* and *condoms* (a necessity even in marital sex in communities with such a high incidence of the disease), the reactions ranged from embarrassed chuckles to tearful nods. Afterward, I was swamped with thank-yous and tearful embraces. I told them repeatedly that it was no great task for a pastor from our sexually explicit culture to talk openly about the church's response to a sexually transmitted disease. But it was a great act of courage, vision, and missional blessing for a small community to inspire so many to action.

The impact of Beacon of Hope has been international. Our congregation in Chapel Hill was one of the sponsors of an outdoor musical festival to benefit the Beacon of Hope. This provided a stage for artists like Jars of Clay and other activists to describe this crisis, tangible ways of response, and the missional nature of the gospel to our city.

Though the emerging church movement is only a decade old, the fingerprints of emerging church plants and missional communities are all over the established church in our culture. In the mid-1990s, it seemed unthinkable to imagine the current levels of artistic expression, new (and old) languages and experiences of worship and spiritual formation, theological dialogue, and missional endeavors in the existing church. Much of this ground was plowed by the nontraditional and experimental church plants that have served as unofficial consultants to the established church over this time period.[110]

Another exciting form of missional community is the new monastic movement. By emphasizing Christianity as a rule of life, rhythmic spiritual practice, countercultural experience, and intentional expressions of peace and justice, the new monasticism is embodying many of the transitions in spiritual formation, community life, mission, and worship that I've discussed in previous chapters. Last spring, Jonathan Wilson-Hartgrove of The Rutba House in Durham, North Carolina, hosted a gathering to discuss the common attributes and elements of the new monasticism. One product of this meeting is *School(s) for Conversion: 12 Marks of a New Monasticism*, a collection of essays offering an excellent description of some of the values of this movement.[111] I expect the new monasticism—just like its historic forebears—to raise the bars of community, justice, and contemplative discipline in the life of the church, as it enters the emerging culture.

The missional entrepreneurism discussed in chapter 9 is another exciting form of missional community. Music venues, cafes, recording studios, advocacy organizations, art galleries, and Web design are just a few of the many types of commercial enterprises (both nonprofit and for-profit) that churches and ministries are encouraging and planting as intentional missional communities. As the growing post-Christian segments of our culture have become increasingly suspicious and mistrusting of institutional Christianity,

---

[110] My personal ministry vision and that of our community has been deeply shaped by the Solomon's Porch Community in Minneapolis, Minnesota. The founding pastor, Doug Pagitt, has been a friend of mine for almost 20 years. I was privileged to watch this community develop from afar and to visit it on several occasions. Doug has given a gift to the wider Christian community by journaling the experiences and values of this community in *Reimagining Spiritual Formation: A Week in the Life of an Experimental Church* (Grand Rapids, Mich.: Zondervan, 2003).

[111] Jonathan Wilson-Hartgrove, The Rutba House ed., *School(s) for Conversion: 12 Marks of a New Monasticism* (Eugene, Ore.: Cascade Books, 2005).

businesses have become safer entry points for community among many consumers in our culture.[112] These cultural changes create a perfect storm for entrepeneurism to become missional and a community expression of the church. The challenging economic realities of emerging culture ministry may make this particular strategy of missional community an essential strategy for providing ministry support, as well as engaging with the surrounding community.

Missional communities offer flexibility, opportunities for cultural engagement, potential resource streams, and no small measure of freedom from some of the programmatic and traditional pressures that existing churches face. These communities are likely to present one of the widest paths into emerging culture.

THE TENTS OF THE CLAN: FAMILIAL PATHS

The early story of Israel in the Old Testament portrays the life of a nomadic people organized into familial clans. Fleeing from Egypt, the 12 tribes of Israel were established. The Israelites eventually end their wandering in the desert and take possession of the land of Canaan, where a nation and a line of kings are formed. Through these historical changes and the future calamities of a divided kingdom and exile, the family clan remained the foundation of daily life for the Israelites. In addition to being the primary economic unit, the clan played a vital role in urging faithfulness to the law and covenants and ensuring the spiritual vitality of the nation.

Families and friendship communities play a similar role in encouraging spiritual health and an ongoing faithfulness to the teachings of Scriptures. So many churches cater to and target family involvement. The signs in front of countless churches in our community proclaim WE CARE FOR FAMILIES! and A PLACE FOR FAMILIES! But while there is more than enough written about parenting techniques and childrearing, far too little is written about the role of families and friendship communities in God's missional plan.

---

[112] The irony here is great. In ages past, many individuals would have been on guard for theft or dishonesty in the marketplace and viewed the church as a sanctuary from these fears. It's not a pleasant reality, but now these fears of manipulation and dishonesty are often directed at the church.

While Moses was receiving the law on Mount Sinai, the Israelites rebelled against God's plan by building and worshiping a golden calf (Exodus 32). Today, I fear that a similar act of idolatry in our culture would be to form a golden likeness of the nuclear family. Threatened by the rapidly changing values and definitions surrounding "family," many church environments seem designed primarily to engage, recruit, and serve families. When this tendency combines with the ingrained consumerism of family life in America, many families assume churches exist to meet their needs. Consider the following mock ad I included in a sermon more than a decade ago:

> Fully intact white Christian family seeks conservative Christian church w/ individualized family educational strategies—reformational theological overview w/ baptistic practice deviation—multiple/concurrent Sunday a.m. worship services each emphasizing folk/blues, contemporary praise, or classical worship traditions w/ hip-hop special music for the kids—targeted outreach programs for all indigenous people groups & Myers-Briggs temperament permutations—meta-church small group philosophy—simultaneous preventive support groups for all possible family dysfunctions with children & youth programming from 7:05-8:10 p.m. on Thursday evenings—in a church atmosphere that accentuates family & Christian unity with no public discourse on fiscal need or volunteerism.

This sense of family entitlement is only heightened when our primary spiritual discourse focuses entirely on personal rather than community spirituality.[113] No wonder many families "shop" for churches in search of the one that best suits their stringent demands, as though they were comparing the features offered by various cell phone plans.

Similar concerns can be raised about our discourse on marriage. In a culture with so many divorces and throwaway marriages, our tendency is to idolize Christian marriage as if it were an "end" in God's plan. Instead, we need to reclaim a language of "sacrament" for

---

[113] See chapter 8 sections on "Sacred Individualism" and "Adding 'Community' to Community Formation."

marriage that describes it as a "means" in God's redemptive work and establishment of a kingdom.

I recently officiated at the wedding service of a couple whose families could trace their generations of Christian commitment practically to the Mayflower. In this service, I described marriage as a two-person drama that describes the character of God, continues and adds to the narrative of God's redemptive work, and builds the community of those who worship God. From the enthusiastic reactions of these families, I could tell I was depicting marriage in a framework that was (sadly) new to them, but also highly motivating.

When families and friendship groups begin to envision themselves as missional communities, the potential for Christian communities to engage and find a voice in the emerging culture expands exponentially. Much of the isolation, fear, and critique that keep us separated from and irrelevant to the emerging culture disappears when we bring a missional posture into the "tents" of our primary family groups. Since families are typically multigenerational, a shared commitment to missionality can encourage cross-generational dialogue that heightens sensitivity to the needs and opportunities of the emerging culture. Some of the most enthusiastic supporters of our emerging culture ministries in Chapel Hill are older people who admit they'd be nervous or defensive about such work if not for their attentiveness to the missional hearts of their children or grandchildren.

For the church to follow this path into the emerging culture, we must expand our concept and definition of "family" and embrace new definitions of family taking shape in our culture. Our preoccupation is often with nuclear families. But with divorce rates exceeding 50 percent and vast numbers of children being raised by single parents, grandparents, or other relatives outside the context of two-parent families, our talk of "family" can exclude the experiences of so many. These family transitions and the instabilities of a mobile, postmodern culture create a great yearning for community that can lead informal friendship groups to take on familial qualities and status.

At the Chapel Hill Bible Church, one reason our conversation about emerging culture ministry has overcome concerns, oversimplified theological dialogue, and the ambiguities of the emerging church movement has been the proliferation of a missional commitment among families and others. Intergenerational engagement has been an ingrained value of our youth, collegiate, and young adult ministries. Ministries on marriage preparation and marriage support have eagerly embraced a missional perspective. Our church's leadership ranks have been filled with women and men who are passionate about missional community and regularly subordinate ambition, status, and materialism to this passion. The familial path into the emerging culture might be the most programmatically simplistic, culturally challenging, and effective road of transition.

THE 12 SONS OF ISRAEL: TRIBAL PATHS

Yahweh gave to the patriarch Jacob the name "Israel," which eventually became the name of the great nation promised to Jacob's grandfather, Abraham (Genesis 32:28; 35:10). In his dying breaths recorded in Genesis 49, Israel blesses his 12 sons, stating that each will have a significant and distinct legacy in the narrative of this nation. Jacob's 12 sons became the 12 tribes of Israel—the organizing geographical, political, military, and economic units of the nation. The unique characteristics and idiosyncrasies of the tribes become rich subtexts in a narrative of the nation.

Like Israel, the church is made up of many diverse tribes who all play a role in shaping its story. Similarly, each individual fellowship is made up of many tribes—tribes based on age, life circumstances, socioeconomics, politics, and theology. Many of the earliest and most popular strategies of ministry transition were tribal paths: an emerging culture ministry (or even a separate congregation) was developed to reach a particular age or affinity group. But some of these approaches were not truly transition strategies. Often, the assumption was that a change in ministry style might attract or connect with a certain population, but ultimately that group would assimilate back into the general congregation as it was. The underlying assumption was that the emerging culture was just a generational phenomenon or an appetite for a different style of ministry that folks would soon "grow out of." Such thinking meant no theological or philosophical reflection was needed to engage the emerging culture.

But some tribal paths can be very helpful in ministry transition. In chapter 9, I described the significance of our young adults ministry in missional transition. I also think transition plans that develop separate worship services or congregations to reach certain affinity groups can be very effective. But such a strategy demands several key prerequisites.

The first requirement is an atmosphere of open communication and trust between the leadership of the primary congregation and the satellite congregation or affinity group. Different ministry contexts inevitably produce misunderstandings and conflicting interests that can be negotiated only on a basis of trust, missional affirmation, and effective communication. Sadly, there are many current church leaders that have neither the level of trust and authenticity required to begin such ministries, nor the sense of security that would allow them to bless other leaders and accept their success. In these cases, this pathway almost always leads to collisions, painful conflict, and blame in success and failure.

A second prerequisite is the creation of intentional points of connection and shared experience between a new or reshaped ministry and existing ministry programs. If the hope is truly to provoke a ministry transition in the whole body, then there must be some means of contact, communication, and shared reflection. Without these intentional connections, even the most trusting environments can sour.

Finally, there must be an expectation of reciprocity and mutual influence. Most "intergenerational" ministries fail when this characteristic is absent. Without the expectation of reciprocity, these ministries are paternalistic rather than intergenerational. The resulting ministry is based entirely on the needs, perspectives, interests, or hopes of the dominant or demanding generation. Similarly, without the expectation that a new ministry directed to the emerging culture will influence and impact the primary congregation, these ministries are often a well-intended paternalism with coffee, candles, and alternative music. When the ultimate goal is to bring the new community back into the status quo perspectives of the existing congregation, it's not surprising that the result is often an expensive outreach to those who could have been ministered to by the existing congregation.

I also believe these tribal pathways have a shelf life and should run their course in due time. At first, some separation of a specific affinity group from a congregation's established ministries is essential to create an authentic ministry environment for the emerging culture. But eventually the old and the new must influence each other, live out the reciprocity mentioned above, and establish a common philosophical ground. In the long run, it's unhealthy to develop communities with radically divergent or competing philosophies.[114] Affinity groups, particularly, should not be developed as long-term change agents. Their purpose is to address the specific needs of a distinct life-stage or circumstance.

Our experience with young adult ministry at Chapel Hill Bible Church illustrates this idea. We formed our young adult ministry from scratch with an emerging culture perspective in mind. But this missional community had a significant impact on the whole congregation. Social justice initiatives, new ministry partnerships, missional endeavors, expectations of multiethnicity, and heightened expectations for community life all grew rapidly. Eventually, we realized we needed to create a "Young Adults Ministry 2.0" that had more traditional aims of a young adults ministry. The young adults ministry as a change agent had run its course. Our next steps in emerging culture ministry would include directing the momentum we'd achieved to church planting and the establishment of more incarnational approaches to the emerging culture. This leads to the final pathway.

---

[114] Remember: I'm not talking about different worship styles here! Many churches have experienced a unified community with a whole spectrum of worship styles. In these cases, there is a common ministry philosophy executed within varying worship styles.

A NATION OF MANY TRIBES: THE PATHWAY OF DIVERSE COMMUNITIES IN KINGDOM PARTNERSHIP

At its best, the nation of Israel was a unified missional theocracy comprised of 12 diverse tribes. Of course, we know the next chapter of that story. The nation fell apart, and its divided kingdoms were conquered and sent into exile. But it was not the diversity of the tribes that doomed the nation into exile and servitude. It was the loss of the spiritual and missional core that bound them together. Unfaithfulness to their covenant with God led to their division and exile.

And, of course, we also know the end of the story. The people returned from exile and reestablished their nation. Post-exilic Israel was the context of Jesus' incarnation and the establishment of the church that carried the message of God's redemption and the hope of a new heaven and new earth. In Peter's great description of the early church as "a chosen people, a royal priesthood, a holy nation, a people belonging to God" (1 Peter 2:9), the greatest legacy of Israel was given also to the church.

Like the early church, and the church in every subsequent historical era, the church today resembles the 12 diverse tribes joined as a single nation to carry the banner of God's redemptive mercy. In our day there is phenomenal diversity among the communities and communions that profess the Christian faith. Despite these differences, there remains a common soul of body and blood, bread and wine, story and Scripture, and testimony and hope that unites us. This reality of the church as Israel's heir, this image of the church as a nation of many tribes, illuminates what might be the most significant pathway of the church into the emerging culture.

I recall vividly a conversation that happened almost a decade ago. I was talking with a group of friends who've become leaders in the emerging church movement. This small circle of friends was filled with emerging church planters, some countercultural voices, and pioneers of new ministry forms. I was one of only two people there who were working in an established, existing church. We were dreaming about what seemed then to be a highly improbable hope for the future—that the values and forms of the emerging church would have a profound impact on the established church.[115] At some point in the meeting, I realized with great clarity that one of the keys to that future would be diverse communities in partnership. In a culture that seemed to be becoming increasingly diverse, multiethnic, tribal, multi-narrative, and decentralized in its understanding of truth, it would be wonderful if the church could embody diverse tribes in community and missional partnership.

At that point, my longing was primarily to see the existing church and emerging churches in vital relationship despite their differences. But now I'd widen my scope to include partnership among all the diversities of the Christian church. Diverse communities in kingdom partnership might be the critical ministry design within the cultural mosaic of postmodernity and the emerging culture.

One story that encourages me involves Warehouse 242 in Charlotte, North Carolina. Warehouse 242 meets in (surprise!) an old industrial building just outside the center of the city. Their worship space is in the former loading dock area of the building, and features metal chairs, contemporary art, and an obvious reliance on media technology. Warehouse 242 is an intentional postmodern church plant of Forest Hills Presbyterian Church, an established church whose own facility and ministry practice is quite a bit different.

A few years ago, Warehouse 242 experienced a season of severe crisis that threatened its existence. During this crisis, Forest Hills stepped in upon invitation, offering the steadying hand and support of a big brother when a weaker sibling is in trouble. In conversations with the staff of Warehouse 242, the established congregation's support was offered without any self-righteousness or smug verdicts about "adolescent postmodern ministries" and their issues. The ongoing relationship between these two fellowships is an example of a unified nation with many tribes.

---

[115] When I look at my notes from these early meetings, I'm amazed at how far this conversation has come! Recent cover stories on the emergent movement in *Christianity Today* and *The Christian Century*, not to mention Brian McLaren's appearance on Larry King Live would have been hard to imagine a few years ago. Even the criticisms that have begun about the emerging church validate the importance of this conversation.

Forest Hills and Warehouse 242 share a common theological heritage. But in recent Emergent gatherings, I've been delighted to see congregations from many different theological traditions come together in worship, vision, and dialogue. I am very encouraged by growing dialogues between mainline leaders and evangelicals.

Our town, like so many others, has long had separate pastors' networks for liberal and conservative leaders. A couple years ago, after our theologically conservative church hired a new teaching pastor, the mainline pastors warmly welcomed our new hire into their fellowship. As this friendship grew, they realized they had far more commonalities than differences. In a similar way, the affection and admiration expressed by Protestants and even theological opponents upon the death of Pope John Paul II offers hope that we are entering a spiritual era of new possibilities.

Sadly, it's still easier to offer stories about division—conflicts between existing and emerging churches, established churches embarrassed by the struggles or even the success of their own emerging church plants, and the painful scars and manifestations of old divisions throughout the Christian community. I believe the effectiveness of the church in the emerging culture will partially be the product of our ability to craft a new missional unity that doesn't demand dissolution of the rich distinctives within our very diverse Christian community, yet also moves beyond the scars and divisions.

In this book I've tried to take on some of the fears and barriers that prevent kingdom partnerships between existing and emerging congregations. I've challenged us to jettison doctrinal gatekeepers that demand theological agreement as a prerequisite to relationship and ministry partnership. I believe it's essential that our theological dialogue on emerging culture issues move beyond generalizations, oversimplifications, and stylized accusations. We'll need to forge ministry practices and partnerships that aren't bound by tradition, personal comfort, or the hegemony of a single generation, ethnicity, or philosophical perspective.

The emerging culture will allow for—and even expect—many different stories and expressions of the Christian message. It's suspicious of homogenous, reductionistic explanations of intricate realities and profound mysteries. Given its yearning for community and relationship, this culture will be alienated if we in the church are unable to dialogue with hospitality and develop partnerships in the midst of our differences. A nation with a shared vision, a common legacy, and many diverse tribes can be our model as we find our way into the emerging culture.

GUIDES FOR THE JOURNEY

The church's entry into the emerging culture is a journey of many paths. I am confident there will be many unexpected sources of insights and inspiration, as well as unforeseen challenges. Yet there are three guides (whose potential for leadership have been championed throughout this book) that deserve special attention: the emerging church, ethnic and multiethnic churches, and the historic church.

The Emerging Church

The emerging church movement has prophetically sensed great changes in our culture and has creatively and courageously attempted to enter this new cultural environment. One of my primary goals in this book has been to help the dialogue between emerging and existing churches so that each could benefit from the other's experiences. But the point has never been that existing churches need to become "an emerging church" in one of the various forms that emerging churches currently take.

Last year at an Emergent gathering, I had a conversation that mirrored many previous conversations through the years. A new church planter had come to the conference desiring to learn more about the emerging church and to fuel his own sensitivities that already ran in this direction. But living in a community that was rural, more politically and socially conservative, and more ethnically homogenous than the urban churches being profiled, he became frustrated. He relaxed when I reminded him that we were not urging him to copy these ministries in his own context. I reiterated one of the primary themes of this book—that the emerging church is not a monolithic template to be copied.

One of my favorite profiles on the emerging church is Doug Pagitt's story of the Solomon's Porch Community in *Reimagining Spiritual Formation*.[116] Pagitt shares the honest narrative of one community's journey into the emerging culture, but never urges others to copy their path. Instead, he invites us to consider what they are learning and what it might say for our own context. When the experiences of emerging churches are examined without the belief that they are inflexible models or a resounding critique of the existing church, they become a great gift and guide to the church as it moves into a more postmodern context. Pagitt urges others to see Solomon's Porch as an imaginative experiment from which other churches might learn. This comment could be applied equally to the great diversity of the emerging church movement.

Ethnic and Multiethnic Churches

Ethnic and multiethnic churches can serve as a second guide. Multiethnic churches exist by definition in multiple cultural realities. In chapter 7, we considered Alan Roxburgh's observation that the church of today exists in an era of liminality between modern and postmodern cultures. As the Christian worldview loses it hegemonic position in our increasingly "post-Christian" society, the church faces greater marginalization, yet greater opportunity to reclaim its intended, radical, countercultural role in society as an agent of God's kingdom.[117] Ethnic and minority churches know all about cultural marginalization. Their experiences have much to teach majority congregations in an era when our faith is increasingly marginalized.

I recently spoke to Anthony Smith, a leader of the Emergent cohort group in Charlotte, North Carolina, about the particular role

[116] Doug Pagitt, Reimagining Spiritual Formation (Grand Rapids, Mich.: Zondervan, 2003).
[117] See chapter 8.

of the African-American church in the church's emerging culture transition. Anthony is an African-American who grew up in black Pentecostal churches. Anthony affirms that African-American churches have much to share with the established, majority church during this era. Perhaps no other church has had a more profound experience in marginalization, isolation, and alienation in America. Many of the recommendations of this book involved movements in theology and practice from the suffocating individualism of our age to more communal approaches. Surely, there is no need to stress the importance of community in most African-American churches! This church survived segregation and persecution by understanding the value of community in both the thought and practice of the church. Anthony and so many leaders with this heritage remind us of the critical, future leadership role of the ethnic church.

Times of rapid or intense cultural change demand that the church carefully study the surrounding culture in order to translate its mission into the new cultural context. Multiethnic churches, ethnic minority churches, and international churches have all had to become experts in cultural exegesis to survive and remain authentic in a world long dominated by Western thought and culture. Their leadership and guidance will be essential as the church transitions in the emerging culture and the voice of North America and Western Europe wanes in the international Christian community.

The Historic Church

Finally, the history of the Christian church can also play a significant role in guiding the pathway of transition. Understanding and study of the history of the church breeds a chastened confidence. We are chastened because we've seen the struggles the historical church has had with epistemological and philosophical transitions. But there is also a measure of confidence as we realize that God's Spirit manages to guide the church through treacherous waters of cultural change. A long-term lens on the story of Christian community reveals that some of our current "theological absolutes" have entered the story relatively late, a fact that should inspire dialogue rather than fearful critique. A longer look at our history reminds us that some of the "discoveries" of the emerging church are, in fact, rediscoveries of values, thoughts, and disciplines that have played leading roles in the historical narrative of the church.

Knowing our own history can also protect us by revealing errors of heart and thought that regularly reappear in the church's story. I believe the church's history humbles us, helps us lighten up, and encourages us to take our challenges and ourselves a bit less seriously. As is the case with that narrative of Scripture, there is only one hero in church history—the triune God who redeems us, reveals goodness and truth, and guides us toward an eternal future. It's a tragedy that so many in the Christian community know so little about our own story. Greater familiarity with our own story will facilitate much better dialogue as we consider changes in both theology and ministry practice.

FINAL ADVICE FOR THE ROAD

When we reflect on the grand story of God's redemption—from the first acts of creation to the formation of the people of Israel to the establishment and spread of the church—it should remind us to be cautious when we use words like beginnings and changes. There is only one true beginning, when God breathed the existence of creation. And there are too many similarities between the journeys of Israel and the church of today to speak emphatically of change.

Nonetheless, there are movements from one season to the next in the story of God's people. There are the great seasonal changes Israel experienced—from slavery, to an inherited promise, to kingdom, to exile, to partial restoration and anticipation. The church has also experienced great seasons of change—theological consolidations, institutionalization, a great reformation, a time of missionary expansion, and now a season where the church appears to be waning in locations of historical strength and growing in lands with shorter Christian legacies. The signs of cultural change and ministry transition are all around us. Time will confirm whether the emergence of postmodernity marks a great seasonal change or a small shift in the weather within some larger season.

But whether this is a paragraph, a chapter, or a whole new volume in the story of God's people, we are in a time of transition. And I believe we are closer to the beginning than the end. This is not the time for confident predictions and bold, inflexible conclusions. It's not a time for church coups ("We must become an emerging church now—or else!") or for congregations that have never before considered the effects of postmodernity to make immediate and radical changes in every area of their ministry. But it is a time for increased dialogue, some wariness, hopeful expectations, and exciting opportunities.

My greatest hope is that we foster a fair, thoughtful, and honest dialogue about the issues, discoveries, and opportunities of the emerging, postmodern culture. I've been concerned that we not succumb to a sense of faddish pragmatism that grabs onto whatever new paradigm seems to work for the moment, "until the next thing comes along." The transitions in worship, spiritual formation, leadership, community formation, and missional expression I've suggested are equally the result of and antecedent to theological, philosophical, and cultural reflection. The transitions I imagine, experience, and hope for are dynamics of both thought and practice.

I hope the stories about Chapel Hill Bible Church have conveyed that the transitions of the past decade have been both exciting and difficult for us. Our leadership has offered us a willingness to dialogue and a freedom to dream that have certainly made us a better church. Sensitivity to postmodernity and questions raised by the emerging church movement have challenged us to make adjustments in our classic strengths of teaching and leadership. These same sensitivities and questions have spurred great growth in worship, spiritual formation, and community formation.

In our particular context, it has been the vision of missional community that has driven our transition and provided the language to make sense of much change. And we have much more to do in the future. Our dream of an emerging culture ministry community and a historically creative, transitioning existing church living in close community seems large and worthy for the times ahead.

Postmodernity and the emerging culture will be experienced differently in every specific church community. Some will rightly realize that faithfulness to their calling and community will mean their transition will come in slow and cautious steps. Others will see transition as an absolute necessity that requires immediate, bold actions. Still others will stand on the steady ground of effective on-going ministries while opening themselves to the new opportunities and possibilities presented by the changing cultural landscape. If we can be kind, bold, and thoughtful in our dialogue with the great diversity of the contemporary and historical Christian community, we will find new creative paths that will allow us to embody and to build Christ's kingdom in this place.

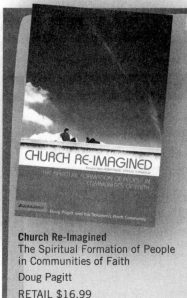

Church Re-Imagined
The Spiritual Formation of People in Communities of Faith
Doug Pagitt
RETAIL $16.99
ISBN 0-310-26975-X

Inside these pages you'll spend a full week with Solomon's Porch–a holistic, missional, Christian community in Minneapolis, Minnesota–and get a front row seat at the gatherings, meetings, and meals. Along the way, you'll also discover what spiritual formation looks like in a church community that moves beyond education-based practices by including worship, physicality, dialogue, hospitality, belief, creativity, and service as means toward spiritual formation rather than mere appendices to it.

Preaching Re-Imagined
The Role of the Sermon in Communities of Faith
Doug Pagitt
RETAIL $18.99
ISBN 0-310-26363-8

What is the role of preaching in the postmodern church? Doug Pagitt takes on this pivotal question as he invites you to reimagine the goals and roles of preaching. Using a few questions as guides, learn how to create followers of God who thrive amidst the complexities of life. Perfect for pastors and emergent thinkers, this book is a hopeful look at the present and future of preaching.

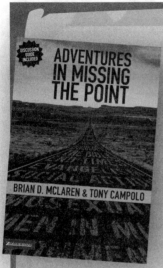

In a sweeping exploration of belief, author Brian D. McLaren takes us across the landscape of faith, envisioning an orthodoxy that aims for Jesus, is driven by love, and is defined by mission. *A Generous Orthodoxy* rediscovers the mysterious and compelling way that Jesus can be embraced across the entire Christian horizon.

A Generous Orthodoxy
Brian D. McLaren
RETAIL $14.99
ISBN 0-310-25803-0

Join this exploration of exactly how we're missing the point regarding hot topics such as salvation, the Bible, postmodernism, justice, and leadership—and what we're supposed to be about. Adventures in Missing the Point isn't about pointing fingers at "them" for their mistakes. It's about us. Professionals and lay-workers, Protestants and Catholics, liberals and conservatives, Pentecostals and Presbyterians—all of us, trying to wake up to new possibilities for the Christian church in the postmodern world.

Adventures in Missing the Point
How the Culture-Controlled Church Neutered the Gospel
Brian D. McLaren
RETAIL $16.99
ISBN 0-310-26713-7

Visit **www.youthspecialties.com/store** or your local Christian bookstore.